Word 2010 Foundation to Expert Guide

Chris Voyse and Patrice Muse

**Published by
Voyse Recognition Limited**

© 2010 Voyse Recognition Limited

This guide has been designed in order to create a methodical approach to learning this product. www.smart-pc-guides.com outlines all the guides in the Office 2010 portfolio.

All rights reserved. No part of this publication may be reproduced stored in a retrieval system, mechanical, photocopy, recording or otherwise without prior consent of the publisher. All trademarks used herein are the property of their respective owners. The use of any trademark in this text does not vest in the author or publisher any trademark ownership rights in such trademarks, nor does the use of such trademarks apply any affiliation with or endorsement of the guides by such owners.

Notice of Liability

Every effort has been made to ensure that these guides contain accurate and current information. However, Voyse Recognition Limited or any associated company shall not be liable for any loss or damage suffered by readers as a result of any information contained herein.

First Published in Great Britain in 2010

Voyse Recognition Limited
Smart PC Guides
Century Business Centre
Manvers Way
Manvers
Rotherham
South Yorkshire
S63 5DA
01709 300188

ISBN 978 1 905657 452

Section 1: Foundation Level Objectives

- Tour of the Screen — 10
- Introduction to Word — 13
- Creating and Saving Documents — 14
- Opening Documents — 20
- Spell and Grammar Features — 24
- Actions — 30
- Format Options Font and Paragraph — 35
- Headers and Footers — 42
- Portrait and Landscape Features — 43
- Print Preview and Printing Options — 45
- Bullets and Numbering — 47
- Simple Tables — 52

Section 2: Intermediate Level Objectives

- Working with Tables — 59
- Section and Page Breaks — 65
- Setting Tabs — 70
- Working with Styles — 75
- Creating New Styles — 78
- Define and Locate Bookmarks — 84
- Generate a Table of Contents — 86
- Creating an Index — 89
- Bibliography, Citations and Plagiarism — 92
- Reviewing a Document using Track Changes — 99
- Comments — 100
- Creating a Mail Merge — 104
- Using Mail Merge to Create Labels — 114
- Templates — 122
- Accessibility Checker — 126

Section 3: Expert Level Objectives

- Outline View — 130
- Master Documents — 135
- Form Design — 138
- Introduction to Macros — 156
- Watermarks — 163
- Hyperlinks — 167
- Columns — 170
- Linking Information with other MS Products — 174
- Inserting Pictures and Graphics — 176
- Drawing Tools — 183
- Working with Text Boxes — 185
- Footnotes and Endnotes — 189
- Shortcut Keys — 192

Note: If you are working in Windows XP instead of Windows Vista or Windows 7, dialog boxes may look different but function in a similar way.

© 2010 Voyse Recognition

Table of Contents

Section 1 9
Foundation Level Objectives 9
Tour of the Word Screen 10
Opening Microsoft Word 13
   Creating a Folder 14
   Creating a Sub-Folder.. 14
Creating and Saving a Document.. 14
   Save a Document as a PDF... 16
Exercise 1: - Creating and Saving a Document 19
Opening Documents using the File Tab 20
   Adding Recently Used Documents to the File Tab............................ 20
   Pin a Document to the Recent Documents Area.............................. 21
   Open a Document using the Mouse.. 21
   Open Documents using the Control Key 22
   Open Documents using the Shift Key 22
   Amend or Delete Recently used Files 23
Spell and Grammar Facility 24
   Adding Words to the Dictionary.. 25
   Grammar Check Facility... 25
Undo and Redo Facility 25
Highlighting Information in a Document... 26
   Highlighting a Character, Word, Paragraph or Document................ 26
Moving Information in a Document 27
   Move Information using the Mouse 27
   Move Information using Keyboard Shortcuts 27
   Move, Drag and Drop Information 27
Copying Information in a Document 28
   Copy Information using the Mouse 28
   Copy Information using Keyboard Shortcuts 28
   Drag and Copy Information 28
Exercise 2: - Copy and Move Functions 29
Actions.. 30
   Checking the Action Settings Option... 30
   Using Actions 31
Exercise 3: - Add an Address to Actions 32
Hard Spacing.. 33
   Creating a Hard Space... 33
AutoCorrect Feature 33
   Opening the AutoCorrect Facility 33
   Deleting an AutoCorrect Entry 35
Format Options... 35
   The Font Group Icons 35
   Formatting Font Group... 36
   Format Menu Options 37
   The Paragraph Group Icons.. 38
   Paragraph Group 38

Format Painter	41
Header and Footer Information	42
Creating Information in the Header and Footer	42
Page Setup	43
Paper Tab	44
Print Preview and Printing a Document	45
Bullets and Numbering	47
Bulleted Lists as you Type	47
Bullet Library	47
Customised Bulleted List	48
Numbered List	49
Continue a Numbered List	49
Restart Numbering	49
Own Numbering Style	50
Exercise 4: - Bulleted Lists	51
Tables	52
Table Grouping Commands	52
Inserting Rows	53
Inserting Columns	53
Merge or Join Cells	54
Deleting Rows	54
Deleting Columns	54
Insert Table Feature	55
Exercise 5: - Creating a Simple Table	57
Section 2	58
Intermediate Level Objectives	58
Working with Tables	59
AutoFit Feature	59
AutoFormat Feature	59
Deleting a Table Style	62
Drawing Pencil	62
Rotating Text in a Table	63
Exercise 6: - Creating a Booking Form	64
Different Types of Breaks	65
Create a Section Break	65
Delete a Page, Column or Section Break	68
Header and Footer: Moving between Sections	68
Exercise 7: - Creating a Header and Footer	69
Identify the Tab Stop Marker	70
Different Tab and Indent Icons	70
Setting Tabs from the Ruler	70
Removing Tabs from the Ruler	71
Setting Tabs from the Tab Dialog Box	71
Exercise 8: - Creating Tabs	74
What are Styles?	75
Displaying Styles in a Document	75
Working with Styles	76
Modifying a Style	76
Adding a Style to a Template	78
Automatic Update Feature	78

- Creating a New Style 78
- Assign a Shortcut Key to a Style 79
- Deleting a Style from a Template 81
- Exercise 9: - Creating a Document using Styles 83
- Bookmarks 84
  - Adding a Bookmark 84
  - Locating a Bookmark 85
  - Deleting a Bookmark 86
- Creating a Table of Contents 86
- Exercise 10: - Updating a Table of Contents 88
- Indexes 89
  - Creating an Index 89
- Bibliography, Citations and Plagiarism 92
  - Add a Citation and Source to a Document 92
  - Add a Bibliography at the End of a Document 94
  - Edit a Citation or Source 95
  - Delete a Citation or Source 97
- Exercise 11: - Add a Bibliography 98
- Reviewing a Document using Track Changes 99
  - How to use Track Changes 99
- Comments 100
  - Inserting a Comment 100
  - Editing a Comment 100
  - Viewing Comments 101
  - Deleting a Comment 101
  - Compare and Combine Multiple Copies 101
- Mail Merge 104
  - Creating Letters using Mail Merge 104
  - Creating Labels using Mail Merge 114
- Exercise 12: - Creating Labels 121
- Templates 122
  - Save a Document as a Template 122
  - View a Template 124
  - Open and Amend an existing Template 125
- Accessibility Checker 126
- Section 3 129
- Expert Level Objectives 129
- Outline View 130
  - Outline Commands 130
  - Outlining an Existing Document 130
  - Promote and Demote Information 131
  - Move Information in Outline View 132
- Exercise 13: - Working with a Table of Contents 133
- Outlined Numbered List 134
- Master Documents 135
  - Creating a Master Document 135
  - Opening a Subdocument 136
  - Inserting a Subdocument 137
  - Moving a Subdocument 138
  - Delete a Subdocument 138

Lock and Unlock Subdocuments 138
Form Commands 138
Exercise 14: - Creating a Form using the Form Commands 139
Inserting Text Form Fields 140
   Inserting Check Box Form Fields 141
   Customising Text Form Fields 142
   Customising Check Box Form Fields 144
   Protecting Forms 146
AutoText Entries 148
   Date Fields 150
AutoText List 151
   Ask Field 152
Exercise 15: - Fill-in Fields 154
Macros 156
   Record a Macro 156
   View and Edit a Macro 159
   Deleting a Macro 161
Exercise 16: - Generate a Table of Contents Macro 162
Watermarks 163
   Picture Watermarks 163
   Text Watermark 164
   Customise a Text Watermark 164
   Delete a Watermark 165
Exercise 17: - Creating a Watermark 166
Hyperlinks 167
   Creating a Hyperlink to a Web Page 167
   Edit a Hyperlink 168
   Delete a Hyperlink 169
   Creating a Hyperlink in a Document 169
Columns Feature 170
Charts 172
   Insert a Chart in a Document 172
   Edit a Chart 173
Copy Information from Excel 173
Paste Special 174
Exercise 18: - Columns, Hyperlinks and Macros 175
Graphics 176
   Inserting a Picture in a Document 176
   Edit a Picture in a Document 177
   Cropping Pictures 178
   Inserting WordArt into a Document 180
   Adding Shadows 181
   Edit WordArt in a Document 181
   Formatting WordArt in a Document 181
   Adding AutoShapes to Documents 182
   Drawing Tools 183
   Drawing Objects 184
   Text Boxes 185
   Linking Text Boxes 186
   Display Text Box Tools 186

- Text Wrapping 186
- Footnotes and Endnotes 189
  - Inserting a Footnote 189
  - Inserting a Endnote 190
  - Amending a Footnote or Endnote 190
  - Deleting a Footnote or Endnote 190
  - Renumbering a Footnote or Endnote 190
- Shortcut Keys 192
- Index 193

Section 1

Foundation Level Objectives

	Page
• Tour of the Screen	10
• Introduction to Word	13
• Creating and Saving Documents	14
• Opening Documents	20
• Spell and Grammar Features	24
• Actions	30
• Format Options Font and Paragraph	35
• Headers and Footers	42
• Portrait and Landscape Features	43
• Print Preview and Printing Options	45
• Bullets and Numbering	47
• Simple Tables	52

Tour of the Word Screen

Word 2010 is a word processing application that runs in a Windows environment allowing the user to create and edit professional-looking documents fast and easy. Its user-friendly prompts help to identify icons on the screen that the user maybe unfamiliar with and takes the user through the various functions within this application.

Tour of the Screen

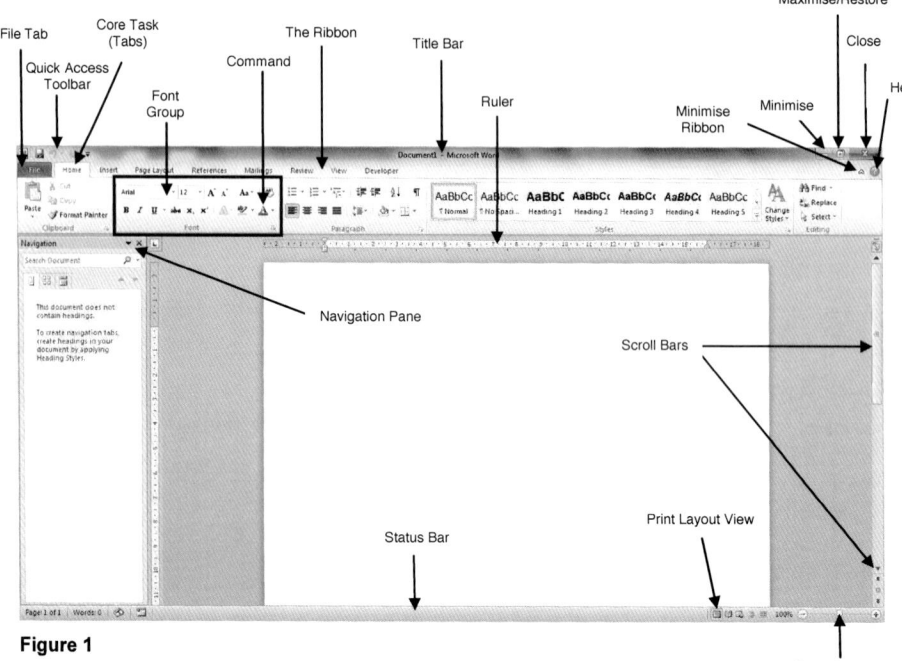

Figure 1

File Tab

In Word 2010 the **File** Tab replaces the Office Button and File Menu found in earlier versions of Word. Clicking the File Tab takes the user to the Backstage view where files and data about them are managed, for example creating, saving and setting options. The File Tab also displays the commands for Open, Close, Info, Recent, New, Print, Save and Send, Help, Options and Exit and the related options available under each command.

Quick Access Toolbar

The Quick Access Toolbar can be found in the top section of the screen. It allows the user to display commands that are regularly used and that are independent of their associated tabs. There is the option to locate the Quick Access Toolbar in two locations near to the top section of the screen.

Help

The Help ⓘ icon can be found on the Ribbon or by pressing `F1`

Title Bar

The Title Bar is highlighted at the top of the screen and defines the programme that the user is in and the name of the Word document that the user has opened. Word will automatically display the default name, for example Document1, however once the document has been saved the name of the saved document will be displayed in this area.

Ribbon

The Ribbon is the control centre to quickly help the user find the commands that help the user complete a task. The Ribbon is organised into three parts:

Core Tasks consisting of seven tabs: Home, Insert, Page Layout, References, Mailings, Review and View

Groups: related items grouped together

Commands: buttons, boxes and menus that give instruction

The Ribbon organises the commands into logical groups all collected together under the Tabs with each Tab relating to a type of activity. To minimise the Ribbon double click with the left 🖰 button on the active Tab, for example `Home`, the Ribbon and its commands disappear. To display the Ribbon and its commands, click with the left 🖰 button on the Tab. Alternatively press `CTRL` `F1` to collapse or expand the tabs.

Ruler

When working in Print Layout, Web Layout or Draft View options, a horizontal ruler is displayed as a default. A vertical ruler can also be viewed in Print Layout View and Print Preview.

Scroll Bars

Horizontal and Vertical scroll bars enable users to move around the document.

Zoom Control

To use the Zoom Control drag with the left 🖰 button to increase (magnify) or decrease the worksheet to display the information larger or smaller on screen.

Navigation Pane

The Navigation Pane is new to 2010 and can help the user find text, tables, graphics, comments, footnotes, endnotes and equations. It also allows the user to quickly look at the structure of a document and change the structure by dragging headings inside the Navigation Pane. The Navigation Pane has three tabs allowing the user to navigate a document by a heading, a page, or search for text or objects. Check the Navigation Pane is switched on by selecting View, Navigation Pane from the Show Grouping.

Status Bar

The Status Bar is at the bottom of the screen. To customise the Status Bar:

1. Right click on the Status Bar, the Customise Status Bar appears
2. To activate Caps Lock to be displayed in the Status Bar
3. Click with the left button on **Caps Lock**
4. A tick ✓ is displayed to indicate the feature has been activated
5. Click back in the worksheet
6. Press the **CAPS** key on the keyboard
7. **Caps Lock** is displayed in the Status Bar to show that it is activated
8. Click the **CAPS** key on the keyboard a second time to switch the feature off

The Status Bar at the bottom of the screen displays the page, section and the total number of pages in a document.

Print Layout View

Print Layout View is useful to see graphics; it provides a fast and easy way for editing information in the Header and Footer.

Full Screen Reading View

The Full Screen Reading View allows the user to hide all toolbars except for the reading layout and reviewing toolbars enabling the user to read the text more easily.

Web Layout View

The Web Layout View is useful when creating a web page or to review a web based document on screen. This icon allows the user to see how features are positioned in web page view.

Outline View

The Outline View allows the user to look at the structure of a document; it also collapses a document so the user see only the main headings.

Draft View

The Draft View can be found at the bottom right hand side of the screen and has replaced Normal View that was available in previous versions of Word.

Opening Microsoft Word

There are several ways that this application can be opened. To open the Word 2010 application, select the Start Button, move the mouse pointer and pause over ▶ All Programs, click with the left button on Microsoft Office; select W Microsoft Word 2010, click with the left button to open the programme.

Drives, Folders and Files

Information is stored on a computer to make it easy for the user to find by organising the information into three levels using Drives, Folders and Files.

A Drive is a physical storage device for holding folders and files. The (C:) drive is the hard disk, other drives may include for example, *depending on the specification of the computer*, the (A:) drive - the floppy disk, a CD-ROM drive, DVD RW and a USB port that allows information to be stored on a portable USB device. If the computer is on a network the user may be able to access the hard drive of other computers via the network drive.

A Folder is the container for the files that are grouped into folders that are easier to find and work with and can be broken down into sub folders. A folder may contain thousands of files.

A File is the computer's basic unit for information storage. Everything on a computer is stored in a file of one type or another, for example

Figure 2

Documents

Documents is a folder that provides the user with a convenient place to store documents, graphics, or other files that need to be accessed quickly. When a file is saved in Word, the file is automatically saved in Documents, unless a different folder is chosen. This is normally the personal drive and displays the folders and files that the user works with on a regular basis.

Creating a Folder

1. Select the Start Button, choose `Documents` to display the Documents area
2. Click with the left button on `Organize ▼`
3. Choose `Layout` ▸ , `Menu bar`
4. The Menu Bar is displayed `File Edit View Tools Help`
5. Select <u>F</u>ile, `New` ▸ , `Folder`
6. The `New folder` appears in the right hand pane highlighted in blue
7. Type Introduction to 2010 in the highlighted area
8. Press `Enter`, to display the `Introduction to 2010` folder

Creating a Sub-Folder

1. Double click the left button to open the `Introduction to 2010` folder
2. Select <u>F</u>ile, `New` ▸ , `Folder`
3. Create a new folder, named Microsoft Excel, press `Enter` to display the folder
4. Repeat the process to create sub folders for Microsoft PowerPoint and Microsoft Word
5. To change a folder's name, right click on the folder Microsoft Word
6. Choose `Rename` to highlight the folder
7. Rename the folder as Microsoft Word 2010, press `Enter`
8. Select the `File` Tab, choose `Close`

Creating and Saving a Document

When a user starts to type text within a document, a flashing cursor can be seen as a vertical black line. This flashes and indicates the point at which the user will start typing. As the user types the text, the text starts to appear from left to right. When typing if the user wants to move back a few characters, the use can either move on the screen by holding down the left button and moving the cursor, or use the `◄──` key on the keyboard. Text moves down the screen as the document is created. The space bar on the keyboard is used to create a space between the words. Capitalisation is achieved by using the Caps Lock icon `CAPS` on the keyboard. Reselect `CAPS` to switch back to lowercase. To capitalise one character at a time, move the cursor to the character requiring capitalisation, hold the SHIFT key down, select the letter to appear as a capital and let go of the SHIFT key to continue typing in lowercase.

1. To open a new blank document, select the File Tab
2. Select New with the left button
3. Double click with the left button on Blank document
4. Alternatively select Blank document, press Create
5. The new blank document appears
6. Type in the document "My First Document"
7. Select File, Save As
8. The Save As dialog box appears

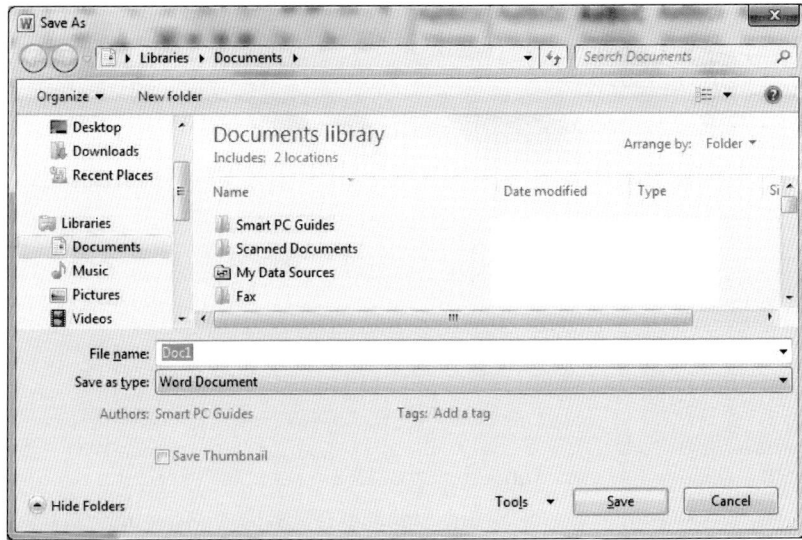

Figure 3

9. In the File name box type Creating My First Document in Word
10. The Save as type area defaults as a Word Document

11. Select `Save`

12. The Title Bar area at the top of the screen now displays the named document as Creating My First Document in Word - Microsoft Word

13. Alternatively press `F12` to display the Save As dialog box

Note: If the document was to be saved to a different drive for example the `DVD-RW Drive`, use the scroll bar and choose `Computer` from the Favourite Links area and select the appropriate drive to save the document.

Save a Document as a PDF

A document can be saved as a PDF (Portable Document Format); that is a fixed layout format and is a useful method of saving a document that is intended to be read and printed but not modified. To read a PDF the user will need to have Acrobat Reader installed on the computer.

1. Select `File`, `Save As`
2. In the File name box type Creating My First Document in Word
3. The Save as type area defaults as a Word Document
4. Using the arrow key scroll down and select PDF

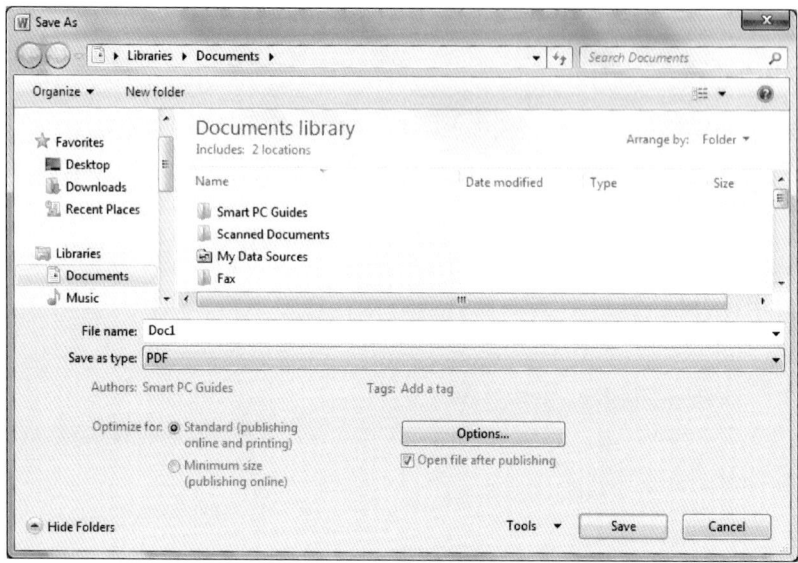

Figure 4

5. Choose Optimise for: select Standard (publishing online and printing)
6. Click with the left button on `Options...`

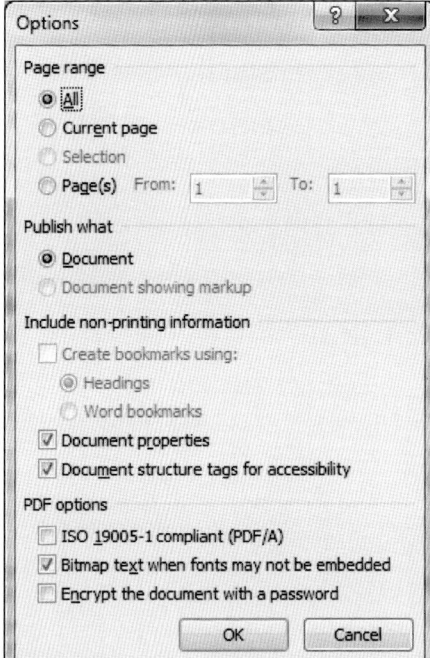

Figure 5

7. The Options dialog box appears showing the default options

8. Select the required options, choose ☑ Encrypt the document with a password if a password is required to open the PDF document

9. Click OK

10. The Encrypt PDF Document dialog box appears

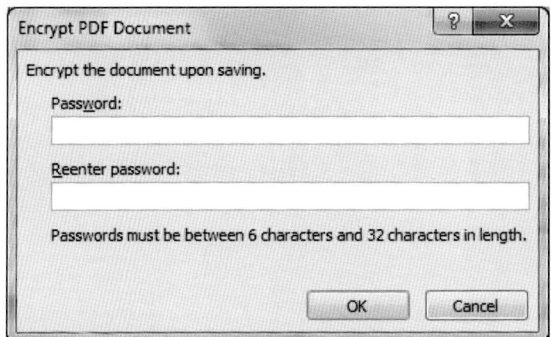

Figure 6

11. Type a password, re-enter the password

12. Click OK, choose Save

13. The following dialog box appears when a password has been applied

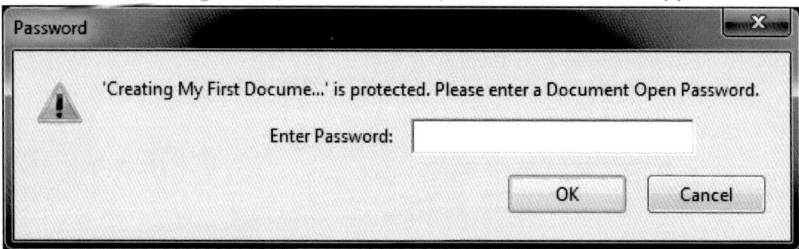

Figure 7

14. Enter the password to open the PDF
15. Click OK
16. The PDF document is displayed that can be read and printed but not modified

Exercise 1: - Creating and Saving a Document

IS IT SCIENCE?

You either love it or hate it! Whatever you feel gardening is the perfect way to wheel away the stresses of the day.

Once you have grasped how a plant works you are in a position to bend it to your will. There are not many plants in the garden that can be left entirely to their own devices and the right time to do a job in the garden is when you have the time to do it properly.

Pruning is the removal of stems, branches or roots of a tree or shrub in order to alter the shape of the plant, to increase vigour or remove dead or damaged parts. It also helps to improve the quality and quantity of flowers and fruits.

Dead heading is one sort of summer pruning we can do that not only keeps the plant tidy but it encourages a new growth of flowers within days.

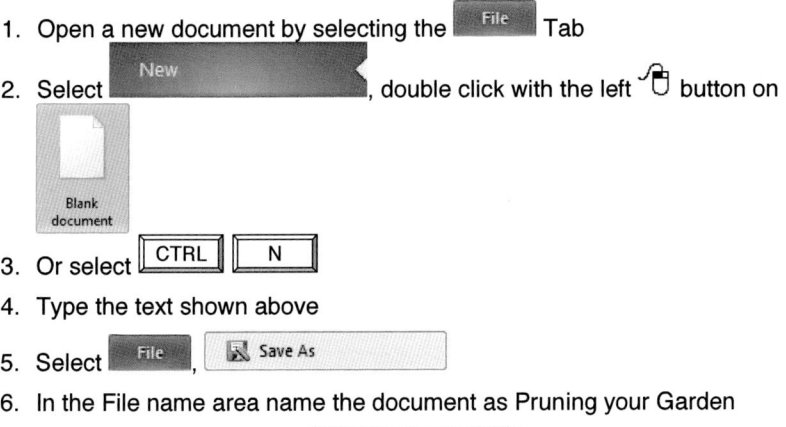

1. Open a new document by selecting the **File** Tab
2. Select **New**, double click with the left button on **Blank document**
3. Or select **CTRL** **N**
4. Type the text shown above
5. Select **File**, **Save As**
6. In the File name area name the document as Pruning your Garden
7. Save the document in the **Documents** area
8. In the Save as type area the default is set as Word Document
9. Click **Save**

Opening Documents using the File Tab

1. Click on the **File** Tab
2. Click the left 🖱 button on the **Recent** documents area
3. The Recent Documents area displays the latest documents used

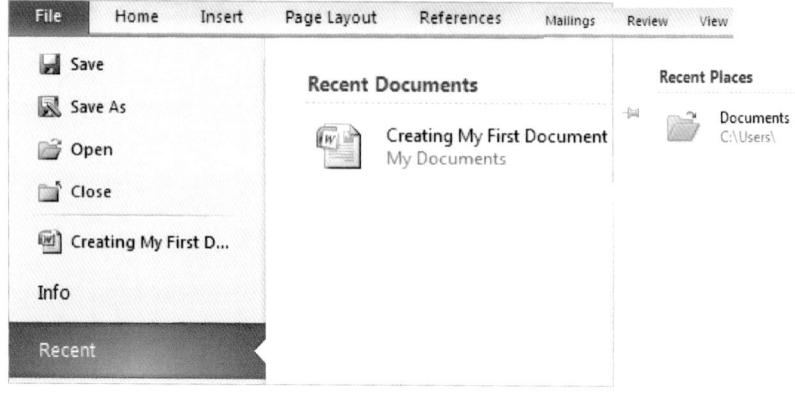

Figure 8

4. Click with the left 🖱 button on the required document
5. Alternatively hold down the **ALT** key, press the letter **F**
6. Use the **→** or **↓** arrow keys to highlight the file
7. Press the **Enter** key to open the document

Adding Recently Used Documents to the File Tab

1. Select **File**, choose **Recent**
2. Place a tick ☑ by using the left 🖱 button in the Quickly access this number of Recent Documents box

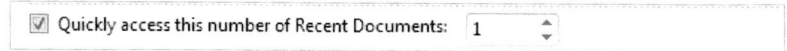

Figure 9

3. Specify the number of recent documents to be displayed by using the arrows

Pin a Document to the Recent Documents Area

The Recent Documents list allows the user to pin documents and folders to the list that the user wants to remain accessible regardless of recent use.

1. Select **File**, choose **Recent**

2. Click with the left button on the pin icon located to the right of the document in the Recent Documents area

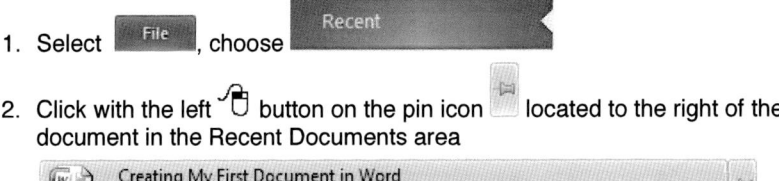

Figure 10

3. The Recent Document area shows the pin has been applied
4. To unpin a document click on the pin icon

Open a Document using the Mouse

1. Press **File**, 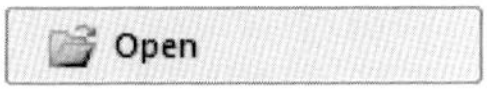 **Open**
2. The Open dialog box appears

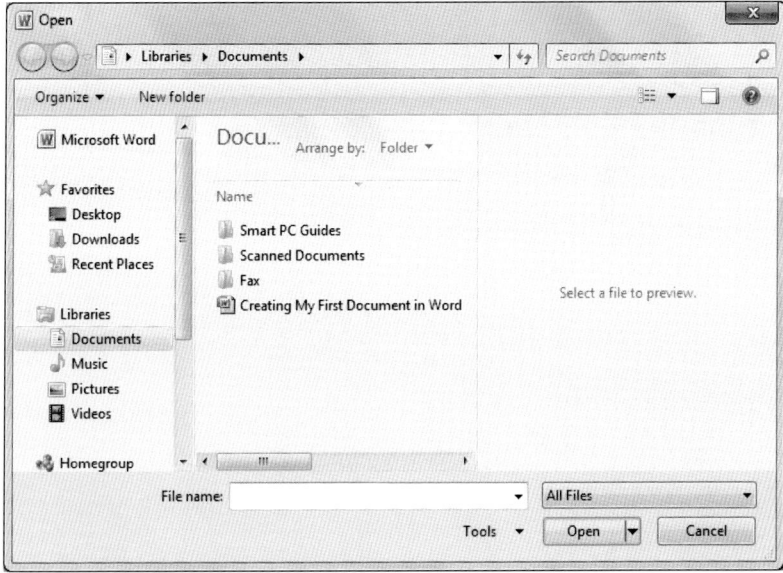

Figure 11

3. Choose **Documents** or the drive that contains the document
4. Double click with the left button to open the required folder
5. Or click the left button on the individual document, press **Open**

Open Documents using the Control Key

1. Select the **File** Tab, choose **Open**
2. Choose **Documents** from the Favourite Links area
3. Double click on the required folder to display the list of documents
4. Click the filename once with the left mouse button to select the first document
5. Hold the **CTRL** key down, click on the next required document
6. Each selected file is highlighted in blue
7. If a file is selected by mistake click again to deselect
8. Click **Open** to open all the Word documents

Open Documents using the Shift Key

1. Select the **File** Tab, choose **Open**
2. Choose **Documents** from the Favourite Links area
3. Double click on the required folder to display the list of documents
4. Click the left mouse button to select the first document
5. Hold the **SHIFT** key down, click with the left mouse button to select the last document
6. All selected files are highlighted in blue
7. Click **Open** to display all the documents

Amend or Delete Recently used Files

1. Select **File**, **Options**, **Advanced**
2. The Word Options dialog box appears
3. Scroll down, choose the option **Display**
4. Select Show this number of Recent Documents:

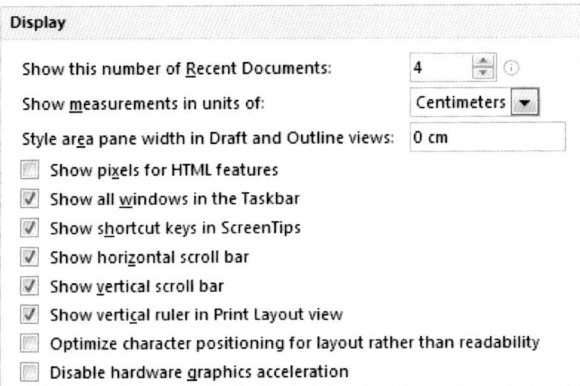

Figure 12

5. Type in the number 10, click **OK**
6. Choose **File**, look below the option **Close**
7. The last document that has been created is displayed
8. Click with the left 🖱 button on **File**, **Recent**
9. The Recent Documents and Recent Places information is displayed

Figure 13

Spell and Grammar Facility

The Spell and Grammar feature checks the text in a document for incorrect spelling and grammatical errors using the standard built in dictionary that can also be customised. If an item has been miss spelt the item has a red underline whilst grammatical errors have green underline.

1. Select the `Review` Tab, choose `Spelling & Grammar`, alternatively press `F7`

2. The Spelling and Grammar dialog box appears if spelling errors appear in the text that are not in the dictionary

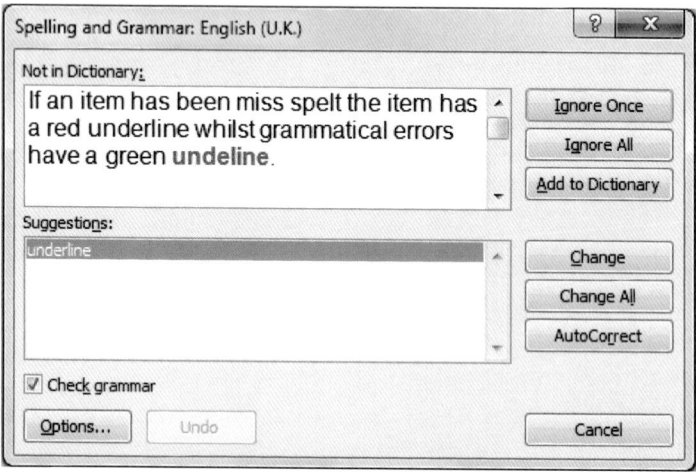

Figure 14

3. The suggestions area gives alternative spellings
4. Choose the correct spelling, click `Change` to replace the word
5. The spelling and grammar facility continues to the end of the document
6. Once the spell check has been completed the following dialog box appears

Figure 15

7. Press `OK`

Adding Words to the Dictionary

1. To add a word to the dictionary, for example a company name
2. Click `Add to Dictionary` in the spell checker dialog box
3. Press `OK`

Grammar Check Facility

1. Grammatical errors are highlighted where alternative suggestions are given

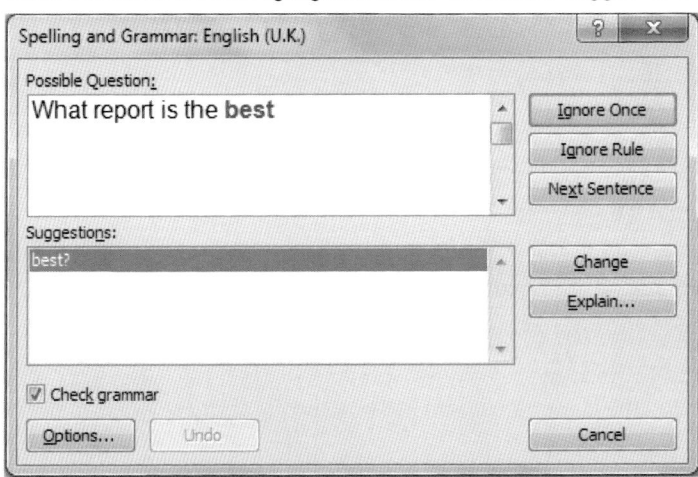

Figure 16

2. The grammatical checker offers the option to ignore once, ignore rule or change the grammatical error

Undo and Redo Facility

When text is entered in a document that information is stored in the memory. The Undo and Redo facility allows the user to either go backwards or forwards on a step by step basis. The Undo and Redo icons can be found on the Quick Access Toolbar located at the top left of the screen.

1. To undo an action click on the Undo icon
2. Repeat the same steps for the Redo icon
3. Alternatively press `CTRL` `Z` to undo changes, or `CTRL` `Y` to redo changes
4. Click on the downward arrow on the Undo and Redo icon to undo or redo a series of changes

Note: If the user clicked on the downward arrow and selected the stage that the user wanted to go back to it will delete all the steps.

Highlighting Information in a Document

Highlighting a Character, Word, Paragraph or Document

Before the appearance of text can be changed, the text has to be highlighted.

Highlight by Characters

1. Position the cursor in front of the character the user wants to highlight
2. Hold down the [SHIFT] key, press the arrow [→]
3. Each character is highlighted in blue

Highlight a Word

1. Position the cursor over the word the user wants to highlight
2. Double click with the left button on the word
3. The word is highlighted in blue
4. Or place the cursor at the front of the word the user wants to highlight, hold down the left button
5. Drag along the word, the word is highlighted in blue

Highlight a Sentence

1. Position the cursor anywhere in the sentence the user wants to highlight
2. Hold the [CTRL] key down
3. Click the left button anywhere in the sentence
4. The sentence is highlighted in blue

Highlight a Paragraph

1. Position the cursor anywhere in the paragraph the user wants to highlight
2. Click with the left button three times in the middle of the paragraph
3. Or move the cursor to the left hand margin, a white arrow appears, click twice to highlight the area
4. The paragraph is highlighted in blue

Highlight the Whole Document

1. Hold down the [CTRL] key, press [A] the document is highlighted in blue

Moving Information in a Document

1. Highlight the information to be moved
2. Select Home, click on the Cut icon ✂ Cut in the Clipboard Grouping
3. The information disappears and moves to the clipboard
4. Using the left button, click where information is to appear
5. Select the Paste icon from the Clipboard Grouping

Move Information using the Mouse

1. Double click in a word to highlight a word
2. Right click, select ✂ Cut
3. The information disappears and moves to the clipboard
4. Using the left button, click where the information is to appear
5. Hold down the right button, select
6. Choose A Keep Text Only (T)
7. The information appears from the clipboard into the selected area

Move Information using Keyboard Shortcuts

1. Select the word by double clicking in the middle of the word
2. Hold down the CTRL key, select X
3. The information disappears and moves to the clipboard
4. Use the arrow keys to go to the new position
5. Using the left button, click where the information is to appear
6. Hold down the CTRL key, select V
7. The information appears from the clipboard into the selected area

Move, Drag and Drop Information

1. Double click in a word to highlight the word
2. Move the mouse pointer over the highlighted word
3. Click and hold down the left button
4. Move to where? appears in the bottom left hand corner of the Status Bar
5. Drag to the new location with the mouse pointer, let go of the mouse

6. The information appears in the selected area

Note: This is a useful way to move information over small distances.

Copying Information in a Document

1. Highlight the information that needs to be copied
2. Select `Home`, choose the Copy icon
3. Click with the left button where the information will be inserted
4. Select

Copy Information using the Mouse

1. Double click in a word to highlight a word
2. Hold down the right button, select Copy
3. Using the left button, click where the information is to appear
4. Press the right button, select Paste Options:
5. Choose the option required
6. The information appears from the clipboard into the selected area

Copy Information using Keyboard Shortcuts

1. Select the word by double clicking in the middle of the word
2. Press the CTRL key, select C, information is copied to the clipboard
3. Click with the left button where the information will be inserted
4. Hold down the CTRL key, select V
5. The information is copied from the clipboard into the selected area

Drag and Copy Information

1. Double click in a word to highlight a word
2. Move the mouse pointer over the highlighted word
3. Hold down the CTRL key and the left button
4. Copy to where? appears in the bottom left hand corner of the status bar
5. Drag to the new location with the mouse pointer
6. Release the left button before the CTRL key
7. The selected information has been copied

Exercise 2: - Copy and Move Functions

The Role of IT Today

The role of information technology has been steadily increasing in importance during recent times. The forward thinking business runs best with the help of modern technology, technology that improves productivity and implements cost-effective business solutions. Powerful desktop microcomputers, which are one application of this technology, can be used for a variety of purposes some of which are listed below:

Preparing and presenting reports by means of word processors

Manipulating large data sets by fact-using disciplines

Analysing complex texts

Developing innovative art forms, both visual and sound

Accessing texts, graphics and data via the internet

Developing valuable keyboard skills

Whatever the area of business, the Role of IT can serve to improve business communications and make life easier for everyone.

1. Open a new blank document
2. Type the text shown in Exercise 2 shown above
3. Highlight a sentence and move it to the end of the document
4. Highlight a word and copy to a destination of your choice
5. Spell check the document
6. Save the document as Using the Copy and Move Functions

Actions

Actions is a replacement for Smart Tags that appeared in Word 2007. Actions allow a user to insert people's names and addresses used in documents to the contacts list in Microsoft Outlook, or to copy and paste information with added control. Word analyses what is being typed and marks it with actions, the type of action depends on the type of data being used.

Checking the Action Settings Option

1. Select **File**, **Options**, **Proofing**
2. Choose, **AutoCorrect Options...**, select the Actions Tab
3. Complete the Actions dialog box as shown below

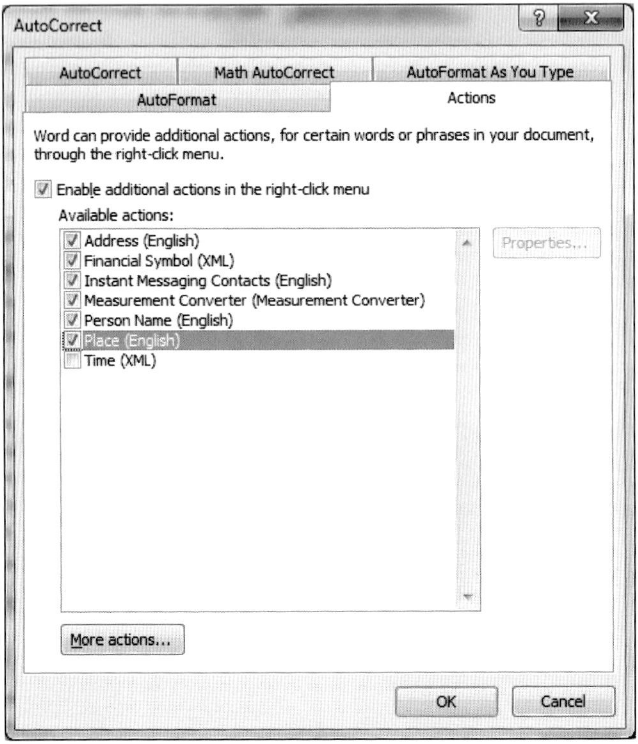

Figure 17

4. Click with left button on Person Name (English) a tick appears
5. Repeat the process for Place (English)
6. Click **OK** twice to return to the document

Using Actions

To use Actions, right click an item to view any custom actions associated with it.

1. Highlight the first name and surname
2. Click with the right button
3. Select Additional Actions, Add to Contacts
4. Complete the Contact Details
5. Click Save & Close to return to the Word document
6. Press CTRL N to open a new document
7. Click with the right button, select Additional Actions
8. Choose Insert Address
9. The address is inserted into the document
10. Once contact details have been inserted, Actions can be used to send mail, schedule a meeting, open a contact, add to contacts or insert an address using the right button

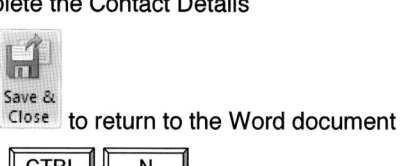

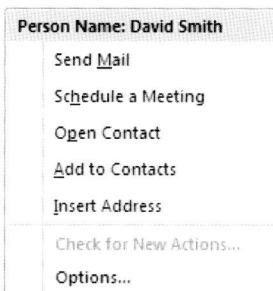

Figure 18

Exercise 3: - Add an Address to Actions

1. Open a new document
2. Type your first name and surname
3. Highlight your name
4. Click with the right 🖱 button, select Additonal Options
5. Choose **Add to Contacts**
6. Complete the Address Details
7. Save and Close to update the Contact Information
8. Reselect your name, choose **Insert Address**
9. The address appears in the document

Hard Spacing

To ensure that names of individuals or organisations stay together, a hard space can to be created.

Creating a Hard Space

1. Select `Home`
2. Click on the Show/Hide icon ¶ from the Paragraph Grouping
3. Type out the name SMART
4. Hold down the `CTRL` and `SHIFT` keys and press the spacebar
5. Type out the name Guides
6. A hard space is shown as a degree sign between the two words
   SMART°Guides¶

AutoCorrect Feature

The AutoCorrect feature corrects miss spelt words automatically.

Opening the AutoCorrect Facility

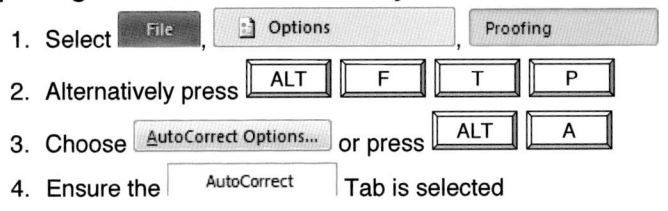

1. Select `File`, `Options`, `Proofing`
2. Alternatively press `ALT` `F` `T` `P`
3. Choose `AutoCorrect Options...` or press `ALT` `A`
4. Ensure the `AutoCorrect` Tab is selected

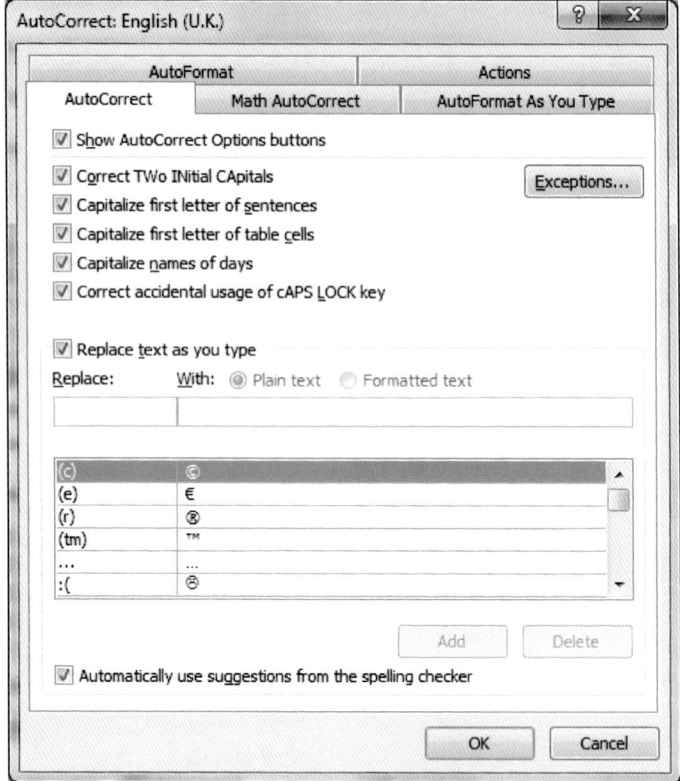

Figure 19

5. Type out sg in the **R**eplace box as shown below

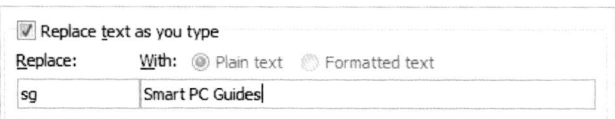

Figure 20

6. In the With box type Smart PC Guides, select [Add], click [OK]
7. Click [OK] to exit the Word Options dialog box
8. Open a new document
9. Type sg (in lowercase) press the spacebar
10. The text Smart PC Guides appears
11. Type SG (in uppercase) press the spacebar
12. Smart PC Guides appears

Note: **If the abbreviation in the replace box was defined in uppercase it would only appear in a document if the abbreviation was typed in uppercase.**

Deleting an AutoCorrect Entry

1. Select `File`, `Options`, `Proofing`
2. Alternatively press `ALT` `F` `T` `P`
3. Choose `AutoCorrect Options...`, ensure the `AutoCorrect` Tab is selected
4. In The **R**eplace box, type the abbreviation to be deleted
6. The abbreviation appears at the top of the list underneath the **R**eplace box
7. Press `Delete` click `OK` twice

Format Options

Formatting allows the user to change the appearance of documents and to maintain consistency throughout documents. Formatting is quick and easy using the predesigned themes or documents.

The Font Group Icons

Icon	Shortcut Keys	Descriptive Prompt
Arial	CTRL SHIFT F	Font Face
16	CTRL SHIFT P	Font Size
A˄	CTRL SHIFT >	Increase Font Size
A˅	CTRL SHIFT <	Decrease Font Size
(clear)	ALT H E	Clear all the Formatting from selected area
B	CTRL B	Makes selected text and numbers bold
I	CTRL I	Makes selected text and numbers italic
U	CTRL U	Underlines selected text and numbers
abc	ALT H 4	Draws a line through middle of text
x₂	CTRL =	Subscript: Creates small letters below line of text
x²	CTRL SHIFT +	Superscript: Creates small letters above line of text
Aa		Changes text to uppercase, lowercase or titlecase
A		Text Effects
ab/		Makes text look like it's marked with a highlighter pen
A		Change Font Colour

Figure 21

Formatting Font Group

Figure 22

1. Open an existing document and highlight the text to be changed
2. Click on the Font Face icon `Arial`
3. Using the downward arrow, change the font to `Calibri (Body)`
4. Click on the Font Size icon `10`
5. Using the downward arrow change the font size to `14`
6. Click on the Font Colour icon
7. Using the downward arrow, choose a different colour
8. The Highlight icon marks text to make it stand out in a document.
9. Choose the colour of highlight by clicking on the downward arrow
10. Select the text requiring highlighting
11. Click on the Highlight icon to switch off the highlight facility

Format Menu Options

1. Select the text to be formatted, click with the right 🖱 button
2. Choose **A Font...**, the Font dialog box appears

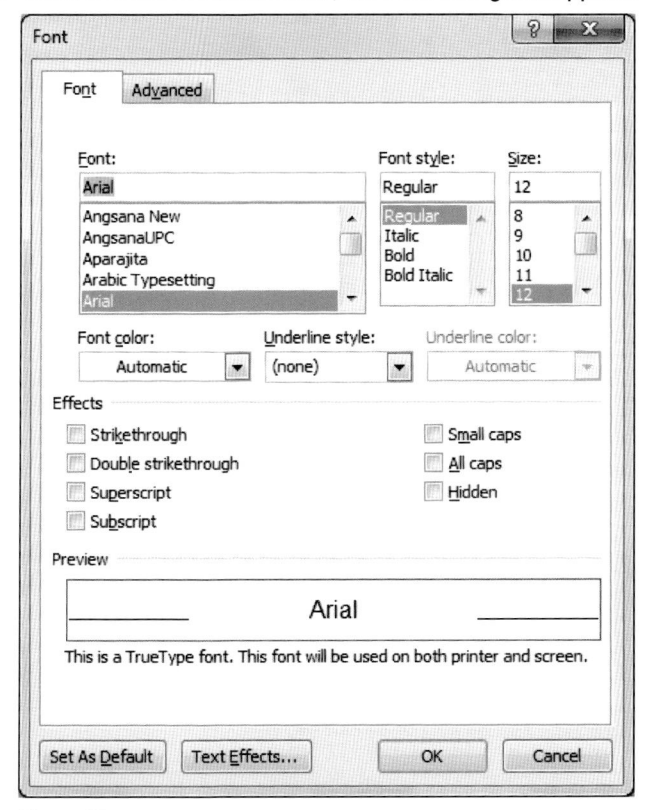

Figure 23

3. Use the downward arrows to select the options
4. The preview area displays how the changes will look
5. Confirm changes and return to the document by selecting **OK**

The Paragraph Group Icons

Icon	Shortcut Keys	Descriptive Prompt
≡	CTRL + L	Aligns text, numbers or inline objects to the left
≡	CTRL + E	Centres text, numbers or inline objects
≡	CTRL + R	Aligns text, numbers or inline objects to the right
≡	CTRL + J	Aligns text to both the left and right margins
↕≡	ALT + H + K	Changes spacing between lines of text
◊	ALT + H + H	Colour the background behind text
□	ALT + H + B	Customise borders of selected text
≔	ALT + H + U	Start a bulleted list
≔	ALT + H + N	Start a numbered list
≔	ALT + H + M	Start a multilevel list
⇤		Decrease the indent level of the paragraph
⇥		Increase the indent level of the paragraph
A↓	ALT + H + S, O	Sort alphabetically
¶	ALT + H + 8	Show paragraph marks and hidden formatting symbols
	CTRL + D	Displays Font dialog box

Figure 24

Paragraph Group

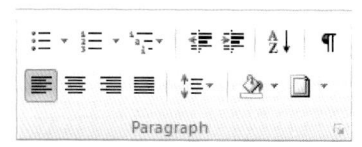

Figure 25

1. Highlight a paragraph to be changed
2. Click with the right 🖱 button, choose ≡¶ Paragraph...
3. The Paragraph dialog box appear

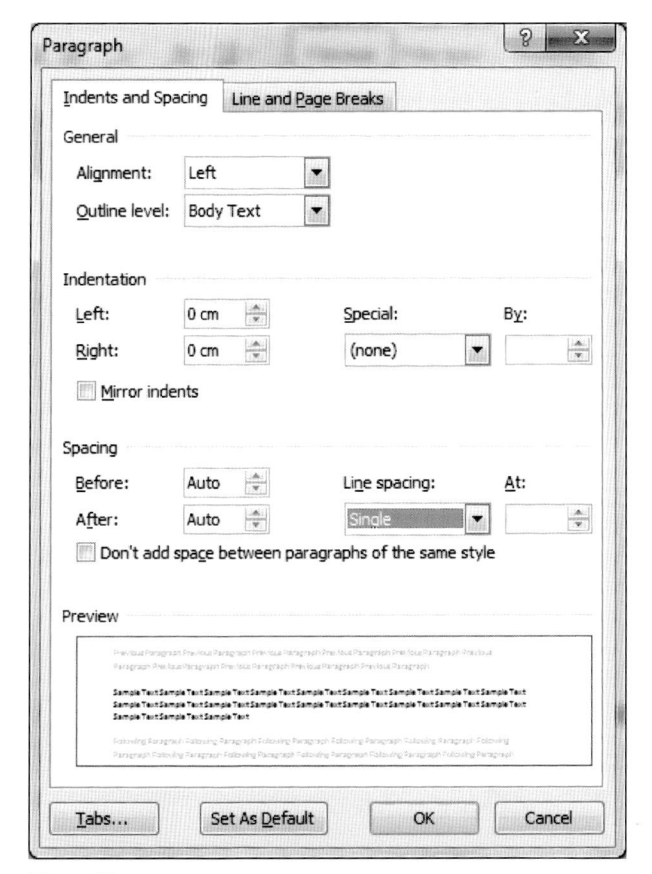

Figure 26

4. The Alignment Box displays the alignment used in the original paragraph
5. To change this option click on the downward pointing arrow
6. Choose the required alignment
7. The preview area displays the amended paragraph
8. The Indentation Box allows the user to change the indentation of the text

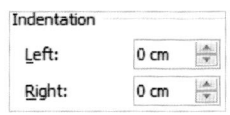

Figure 27

9. Select the arrows and choose the indentation required
10. Preview displays the position of the changed paragraph

11. The **S**pecial Feature Box allows the user to create different Indents

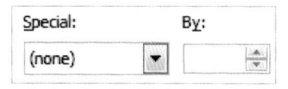

Figure 28

12. Select First Line Indent, the preview area displays the style of indent
13. Choose Hanging Indent
14. To accept any changes, click OK
15. The Line and **P**age Breaks Tab covers the following options

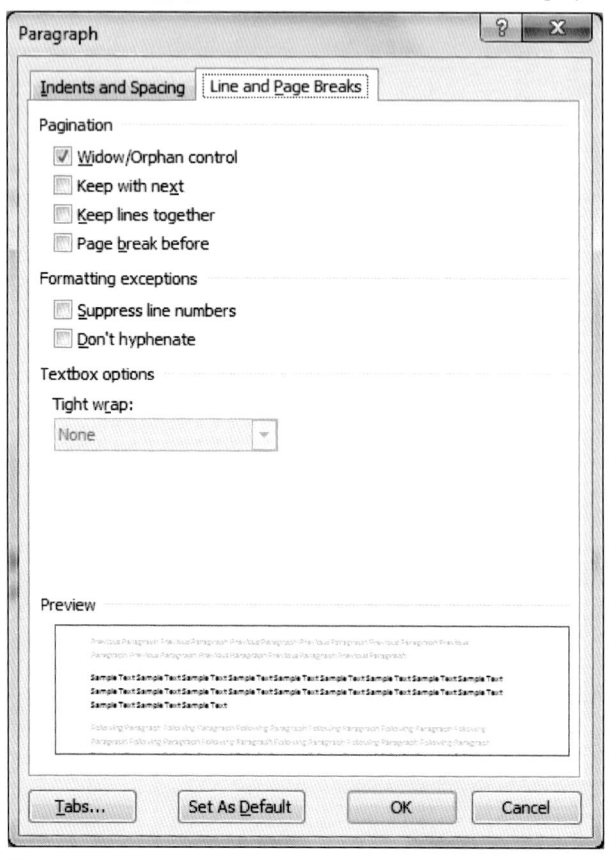

Figure 29

Widow/Orphan Control

The Widow Control sends a single sentence to the next page leaving the remainder of the paragraph on the previous page. Orphan Control leaves sentences while the rest of the text is on the next page. The default is to switch the **W**idow/Orphan control on.

Keep Lines Together

If a paragraph is highlighted using the **K**eep lines together option the paragraph will not be split up by a page break.

Keep with Next Option

The Keep with ne**x**t option keeps highlighted paragraphs together.

Page Break Before

Page **b**reak before is normally applied to headings to force the page break before a selected paragraph.

Suppress Line Numbers

Suppress line numbers prevents line numbers from appearing next to selected paragraphs where line numbers have been set.

Text Wrap

Text wrap allows text to be wrapped around pictures, shapes and tables, choosing any style or position required.

Format Painter

Using the *Format Painter* icon allows users to copy formatting from one place and apply it to another.

1. Select the text to be copied
2. Choose the Home Tab
3. Move the mouse pointer to the Format Painter icon *Format Painter*
4. Double click on *Format Painter* to copy the format
5. When the Format Painter icon is switched on it is displayed in orange
6. Click with the left button on the text the format needs to be applied to
7. The text is changed to match the selected format
8. Switch *Format Painter* off by selecting the icon again

Header and Footer Information

Headers and Footers in a document allow the user to insert text that appears at the top or bottom of every page. The header and footer groupings can be found under the `Insert` Tab.

Figure 30

Creating Information in the Header and Footer

To create information in the header and footer, for example a company name or page numbers

1. Open a document, select `Insert`
2. Choose `Header` from the Header and Footer Group, select `Edit Header`
3. The header box appears at the top of your document
4. Type Smart PC Guides next to the flashing cursor
5. Choose `Footer`, `Edit Footer`, the footer box appears at the bottom of the document
6. Type your first and second name next to the flashing cursor
7. Press `TAB` on the keyboard to move to the centre of the footer
8. Select `Page Number`, `Bottom of Page` to expand the menu
9. Using the downward arrow key, choose `Page X of Y`

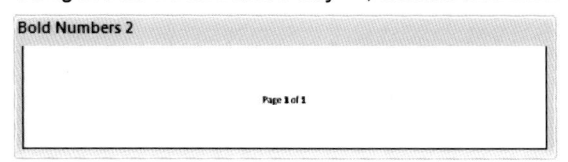

Bold Numbers 2

Page 1 of 1

Figure 31

10. The page number appears at the foot of the page, select `Close Header and Footer`

Page Setup

The Page Setup Group is found under the `Page Layout` Tab and enables a user to define the Margins, Paper and Layout of a document.

1. Click on the `Page Layout` Tab, choose `Margins` from the Page Setup Group
2. Select `Custom Margins...`, the Page Setup dialog box appears

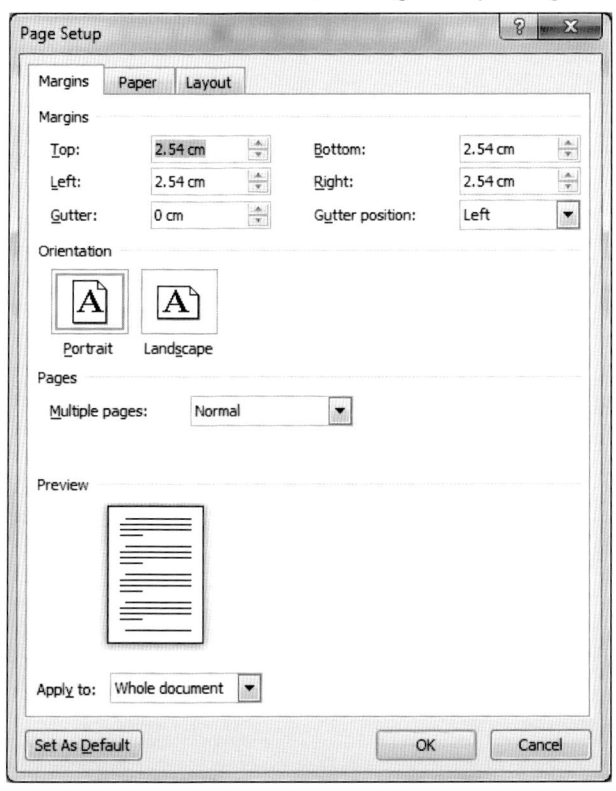

Figure 32

3. Use the arrow keys to change the default margins **T**op, **B**ottom, **L**eft, **R**ight and **G**utter as required
4. The **G**utter margin facility creates extra space when binding documents
5. Change the page layout by selecting Portrait or Landscape
6. Press the downward arrow in the Appl**y** to area
7. Select this point forward or the whole document, click `OK`

Paper Tab

The Paper Tab allows the user to set the paper size or define a custom style.

1. Click on the `Page Layout` Tab, choose `Size` from the Page Setup Group
2. Select `More Paper Sizes...`, the Page Setup dialog box appears

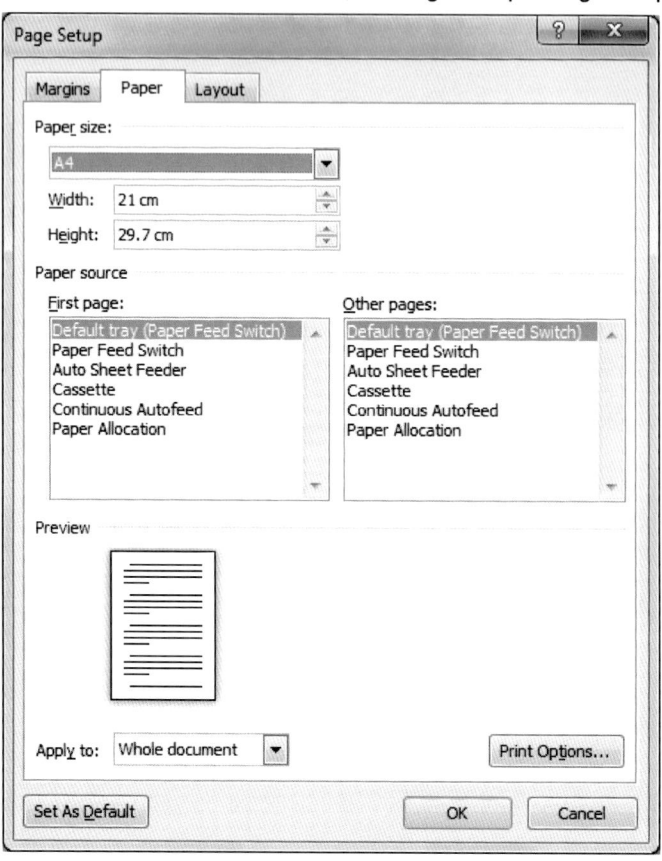

Figure 33

3. Select the required Paper size using the downward arrow
4. The Apply to area enables the user to select whether the amended features relate to this section, this point forward or the whole document
5. Click `OK`

Print Preview and Printing a Document

2010 now allows the user to preview, review, change printer properties and print a document from the same location.

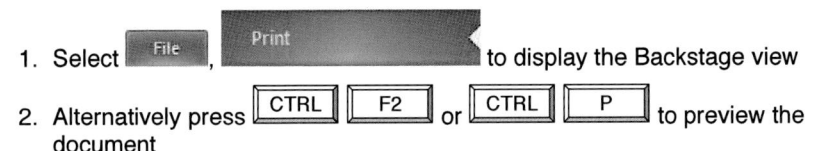

1. Select **File**, **Print** to display the Backstage view
2. Alternatively press **CTRL** **F2** or **CTRL** **P** to preview the document
3. Click with the left button on the Zoom to Page icon positioned in the bottom right corner of the screen
4. A full page is displayed in the preview area

Figure 34

5. Use the Zoom In feature to increase or decrease the preview area
6. Click with the left button on the plus or minus signs
7. Or click on the marker and drag to the required setting
8. To display more than one page decrease the settings
9. Click with the left button to select a different page in preview
10. A light orange border appears around the page to define the page had been selected
11. For more than one page use the next page icon located at the centre bottom of the screen
12. Press the previous page icon to go back a page
13. Use the left button to move the vertical/horizontal scroll bars to view the page
14. The current page and total number of pages are displayed below the preview area
15. Select **Page Setup** to customise the settings as required, press **OK**
16. The current printer is displayed in the printer area
17. Select the downward arrow to choose an alternative printer

18. Choose the settings required for the document, for example print a number of pages

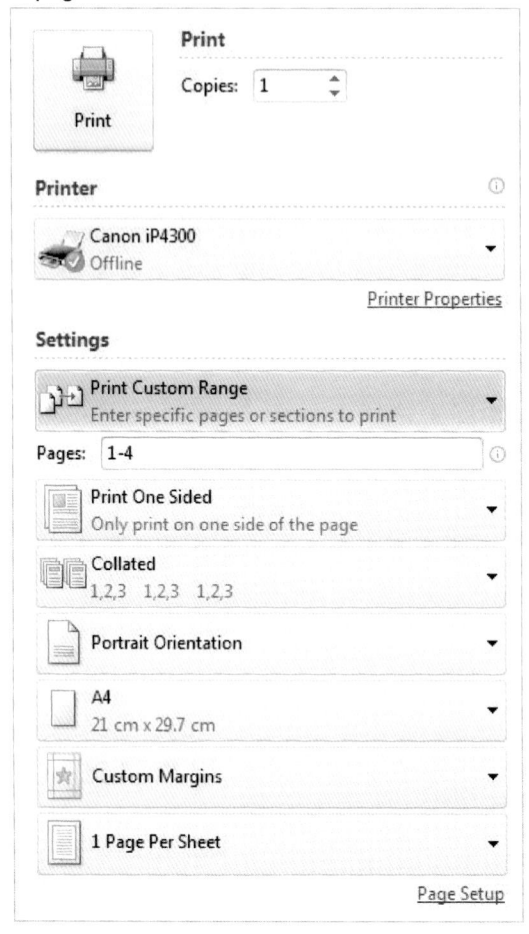

Figure 35

19. Select ![Print] to print the document

Bullets and Numbering

Bullets are a useful way in which to create a list of items in a document.

Bulleted Lists as you Type

1. Click on the Bullets icon from the Paragraph Grouping
2. Type out the first item in the list
3. Press return or Enter, type out the next item
4. Press return or Enter
5. Click to deselect the bulleting

Bullet Library

1. Select from the Paragraph Grouping
2. Click on the downward arrow to bring up the Bullet Library

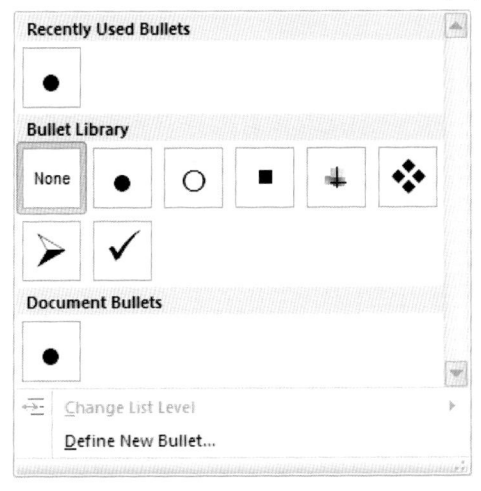

Figure 36

3. Click on the required bullet to return to the document
4. Type out the first item in the list
5. Press return or Enter, type out the next item
6. Press return or Enter
7. Click to deselect bulleting

Customised Bulleted List

1. Select the Bullets icon from the Paragraph Grouping
2. Choose a bullet style, re-select the Bullets icon
3. Click on the downward arrow to bring up the Bullet Library

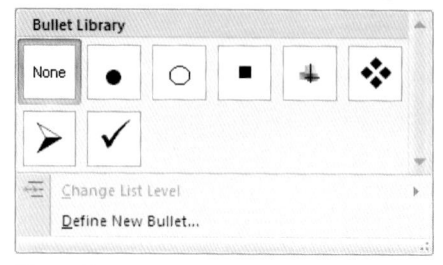

Figure 37

4. Select **Define New Bullet...**
5. The Define New Bullet dialog box appears

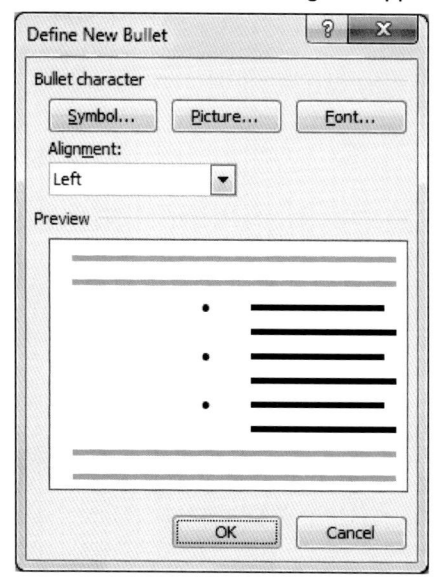

Figure 38

6. Select **Font...** to change the colour of the bullet
7. Click **OK** twice to return to the document
8. Type out the bulleted list, press **Enter** twice to turn off the bulleted style

Numbered List

1. Click on the Numbering icon [icon] from the Paragraph Grouping
2. Type out the first item in the list, press return or [Enter]
3. Type out the next item, press return or [Enter]
4. Click [icon] to deselect the numbering

Continue a Numbered List

1. Select the position where the numbered list is to continue
2. Select [icon] from the Paragraph Grouping
3. Click the downward arrow [icon] to select the Numbering Library
4. Select [icon] Set Numbering Value...
5. The Set Numbering Value dialog box appears

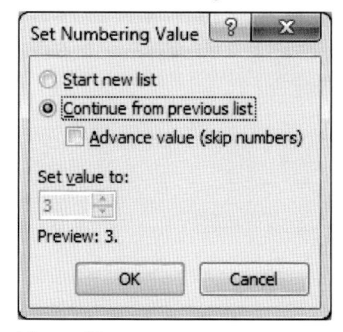

Figure 39

6. Choose [○ Continue from previous list], click [OK]

Restart Numbering

1. Select the position where the numbered list is to continue
2. Select [icon] from the Paragraph Grouping
3. Click on the downward arrow [icon] to select the Numbering Library
4. Select [icon] Set Numbering Value...
5. The Set Numbering Value dialog box appears

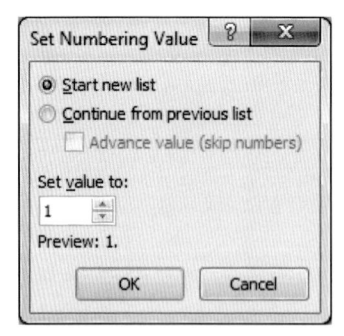

Figure 40

6. Click **S**tart new list, press [OK]
7. Alternatively select the position where the numbered list is to continue
8. Choose [icon] from the Paragraph Grouping
9. An AutoCorrect Options icon appears next to the number
10. Move the mouse pointer over [AutoCorrect Options]
11. Click on the downward pointing arrow with the left button
12. Select [Continue Numbering], or click again with the left button on the downward pointing arrow
13. Select [Restart Numbering] to restart the numbering

Own Numbering Style

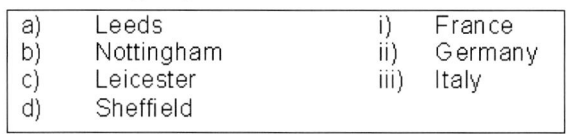

a)	Leeds	i)	France
b)	Nottingham	ii)	Germany
c)	Leicester	iii)	Italy
d)	Sheffield		

Figure 41

1. Choose one of the above styles or a style of your choice
2. In a new document create a list by typing out
   a) Leeds, or i) France, or a style of your own
3. Press [Enter] to move down a line, continue typing the list
4. Press [Enter] twice to turn off the style

Exercise 4: - Bulleted Lists

New Zealand

New Zealand is known as a land of beauty, offering the visitor the excitement of its cosmopolitan cities to the tranquillity of its mountains and landscapes. Positioned amongst the Pacific to the east and the Tasman Sea to the west, New Zealand experiences warm moist climates, the volcanoes in the centre of the islands are occasionally active.

But it's not only the country that's beautiful, New Zealand has beautiful people. With a mixed population, one third of the people are Polynesian, the Maori culture of wood carving, weaving and music can be seen everywhere. The people are young more than half are less than 30 years old. Sheep and cattle ranching is the biggest business with three cattle and 20 sheep to every human.

Auckland with its cosmopolitan atmosphere has high-rise buildings towering over the city and is an important distribution centre. New Zealand is also one of the biggest exporters of seafood and the second biggest exporter of wool as well as exporting Kiwi fruits, oranges and lemons. New Zealand exports more dairy products and lamb than any other nation.

1. Type the text shown above
2. Centre and Underline the heading
3. Change the heading Font to Times New Roman with a Font size of 18
4. Ensure the words New Zealand throughout the text have hard spaces
5. Create a bulleted list at the end of the document of items exported by New Zealand
6. Spell check the document
7. Create a centred Header stating the name of your organisation
8. Create a Footer with your name on the left and today's date on the right
9. Use Print Preview to view the document
10. Save and close the document

Tables

Two quick ways to create a table within a document is by using the Table Grouping commands or by using the Insert Table feature.

Table Grouping Commands

1. Open a new document
2. Click the left 🖱 button in the document where the table needs to appear
3. Select `Insert`, choose `Table` from the Tables Grouping
4. The Insert Table menu appears

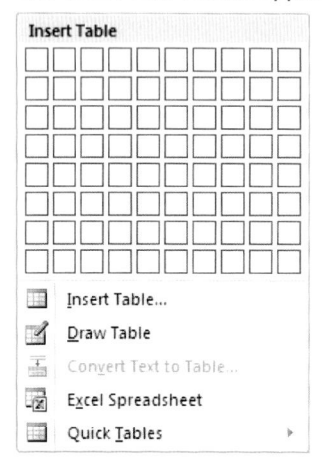

Figure 42

5. Using the mouse highlight the number of columns and rows required

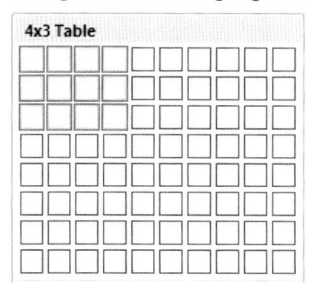

Figure 43

6. Let go of the mouse to install the table in the document

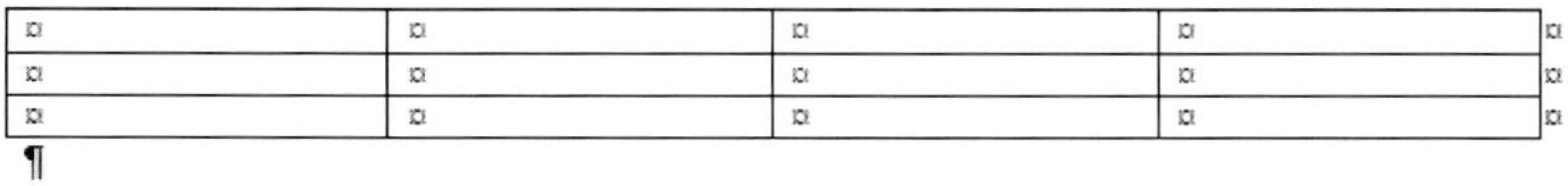

7. Press the `TAB` key to move from cell to cell within the table
8. To move back a cell press the `SHIFT` and `TAB` keys
9. Alternatively move using the keys on the keyboard `↑` `↓` `→` `←`
10. Press the `TAB` key to insert a row at the end of the table

Figure 44

Inserting Rows

1. Click with the right button in a cell where a row is to be inserted
2. Choose `Insert` to expand the menu

   - Insert Columns to the Left
   - Insert Columns to the Right
   - Insert Rows Above
   - Insert Rows Below
   - Insert Cells...

   Figure 45

3. Select `Insert Rows Above` with the left button or `Insert Rows Below`, a new row is inserted

Inserting Columns

1. Click with the right button in a cell where a column is to be inserted
2. Choose `Insert` to expand the menu

   - Insert Columns to the Left
   - Insert Columns to the Right
   - Insert Rows Above
   - Insert Rows Below
   - Insert Cells...

   Figure 46

3. Select `Insert Columns to the Left` with the left button or `Insert Columns to the Right`, a new column is inserted

Merge or Join Cells

1. Click with the right button in the first cell of the table
2. Hold the `SHIFT` key down, click in the last cell that requires to be merged
3. Click with the right button, select `Merge Cells`
4. The selected cells are merged into one cell

Deleting Rows

1. Click in the row to be deleted
2. Press the right button, select `Delete Cells...`
3. The Delete Cells dialog box appears

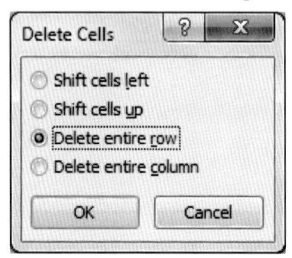

Figure 47

4. Select `Delete entire row`, press `OK`

Deleting Columns

1. Click in the column to be deleted
2. With the right button select `Delete Cells...`
3. The Delete Cells dialog box appears

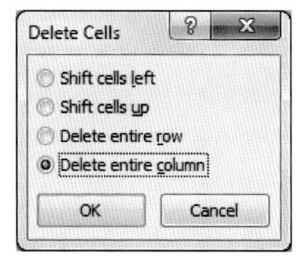

Figure 48

4. Select `Delete entire column`, press `OK`

Insert Table Feature

1. Click in the document where the table is to appear
2. Select `Insert`, choose `Table` from the Tables Grouping
3. The Insert Table menu appears

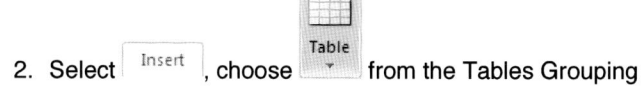

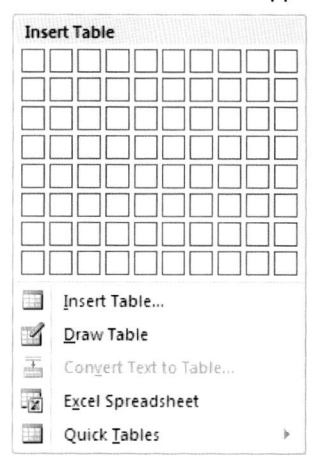

Figure 49

4. Select `Insert Table...` with the left button
5. The Insert Table dialog box appears

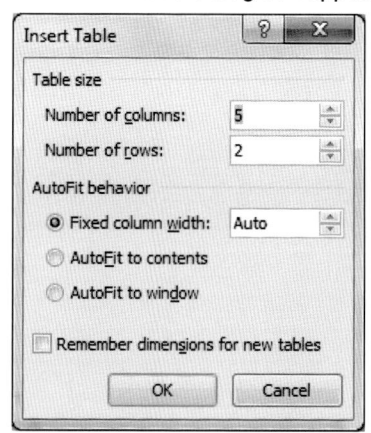

Figure 50

6. Enter the Number of **c**olumns and **r**ows for the required table
7. Select Fixed column **w**idth, choose Auto
8. Press `OK`

9. Select a style from the Table Styles Grouping
10. Extend the menu by clicking on the downward arrow

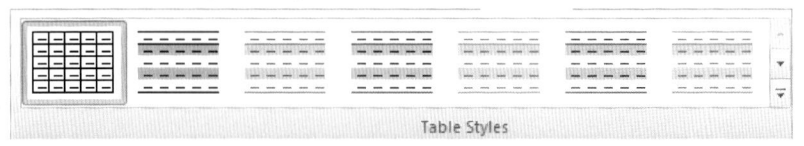

Figure 51

11. The selected style appears in your document

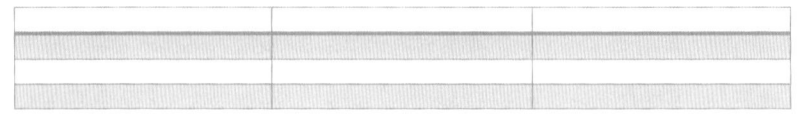

Figure 52

Exercise 5: - Creating a Simple Table

Product	Price £
Garden Peas	0.85
Coke	1.27
Lettuce	0.69
Tomatoes	0.99
Potatoes	0.62
Yoghurt	0.37
Cherries	1.23
Lamb Chops	5.00
Bananas	1.10
Corn Flakes	1.65
Total	**£13.77**

1. Produce the above table using any format
2. Insert a row between Garden Peas and Coke and add Apples at 0.59
3. Delete Corn Flakes from the list
4. Insert a new column to the right of the table
5. Name the column "Use By Date"
6. Find three fruits and replace them with ones of your choice
7. Choose a different style and update the table
8. Insert a Row at the beginning of the table, merge the cells
9. Name the row "Shopping List", highlight and centre the text
10. Save the document

Section 2
Intermediate Level Objectives

	Pages
• Working with Tables	59
• Section and Page Breaks	65
• Setting Tabs	70
• Working with Styles	75
• Creating New Styles	78
• Define and Locate Bookmarks	84
• Generate a Table of Contents	86
• Creating an Index	89
• Bibliography, Citations and Plagiarism	92
• Reviewing a Document using Track Changes	99
• Comments	100
• Creating a Mail Merge	104
• Using Mail Merge to Create Labels	114
• Templates	122
• Accessibility Checker	126

Working with Tables

AutoFit Feature

The AutoFit Feature automatically resizes rows and columns to the size of their contents.

1. Click anywhere inside the table
2. Select `Layout` from the `Table Tools` Grouping
3. Choose `AutoFit` to expand the menu

- AutoFit Contents
- AutoFit Window
- Fixed Column Width

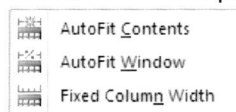

Figure 53

4. Select `AutoFit Contents` to automatically adjust the cells to fit the contents

AutoFormat Feature

The AutoFormat Feature allows the user to quickly customise a table to suit individual needs.

1. Select the table requiring formatting
2. Choose `Design` from the `Table Tools` Grouping
3. Select the Table Styles Command

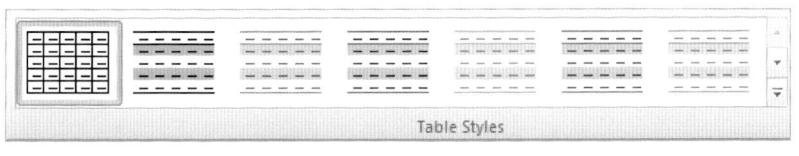

Figure 54

4. Click on the downward pointing arrow to expand the menu

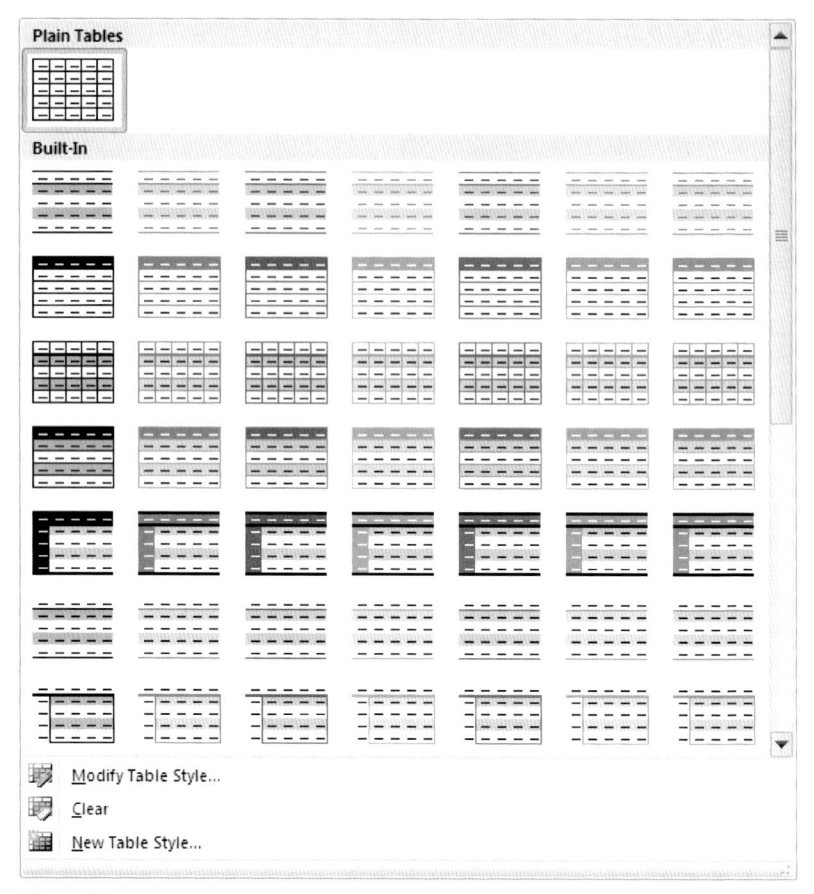

Figure 55

5. Select a style of your choice
6. Select the Table Styles Command, click on the downward pointing arrow to expand the menu
7. Choose Modify Table Style...
8. The Modify Style dialog appears

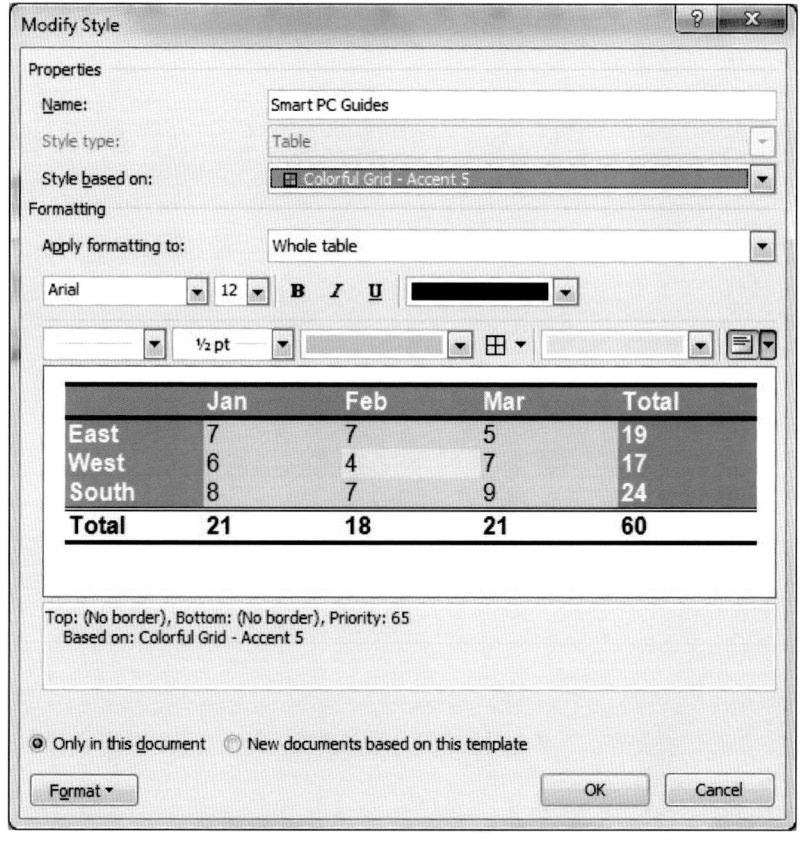

Figure 56

9. Choose **N**ame: and type Smart PC Guides

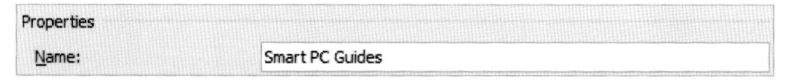

Figure 57

10. Change the Font style to Arial and format the table as required
11. Select the option Only in this **d**ocument or New documents based on this template

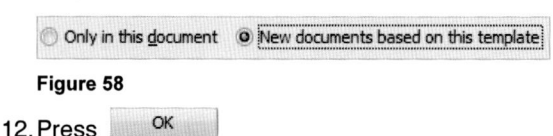

Figure 58

12. Press OK

Deleting a Table Style

1. Choose `Design`
2. Click on the downward pointing arrow ▼ to expand the Table Styles menu
3. Move the mouse pointer over Custom, Smart PC Guides appears

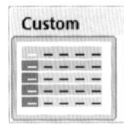

Figure 59

4. Click with the right button, select `Delete Table Style`
5. The following prompt appears

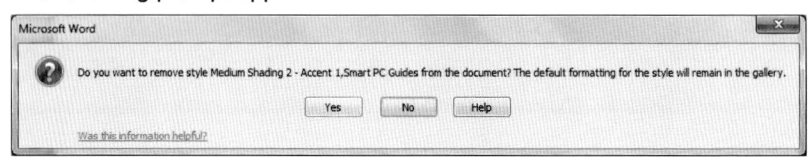

Figure 60

6. Press `Yes`

Drawing Pencil

1. Select `Table`, click with the left button on the downward arrow of the Table command
2. Choose `Draw Table`
3. The drawing pencil appears
4. In the status bar the following prompt appears

   `Click and drag to create table and to draw rows, columns and borders.`

   Figure 61

5. Drag using the left button to create a table by drawing rows and columns
6. The `Table Tools` Tab appears as the table is being created
7. To format, change the line colour, or use the Eraser, select the appropriate command from the Draw Borders Grouping

Figure 62

8. Alternatively use [ALT] [N] [T] [D] to display the drawing pencil

Rotating Text in a Table

To change text direction within selected cells

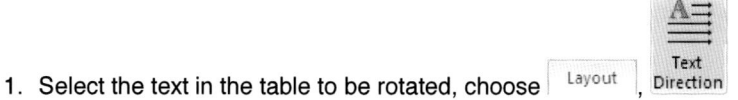

1. Select the text in the table to be rotated, choose Layout, Text Direction
2. To merge cells, highlight the cells in the table to be merged together
3. Select Merge Cells
4. To split cells, click in the cell to be split into smaller rows or columns
5. Choose Split Cells, the Split Cells dialog box appears

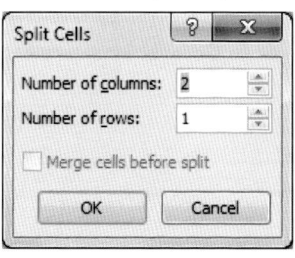

Figure 63

6. Enter the number of columns or rows, click OK
7. To delete lines from the table, select Design, choose Eraser
8. Click and drag with the left button on the line to be deleted
9. Release the left button
10. To switch off the Eraser click with the left button on Eraser
11. To sort items alphabetically or numerically select Layout, Sort
12. The Sort dialog box appears, select the required format, press OK

Exercise 6: - Creating a Booking Form

Smart PC Guides Travel Services				
Departure Information				
Reservation Reference:		Destination		
UK Departure Airport		Name of Airport		
Date of Travel				
Number of Nights				

Title	Initial	Surname (in Capitals)		Insurance	
				Yes	
				Yes	Delete YES if you have arranged alternative insurance which is valid for your travel dates
				Yes	
				Yes	
				Yes	
				Yes	NAME OF INSURER:
				Yes	
				Yes	
				Yes	
				Yes	

Arrival Date	Hotel Name	Resort	No of Nights

Full Address and Telephone Number of First Named Adult	
	Telephone Number
Signed	Date

1. Create the above Booking Form using Tables
2. Save the form as Smart PC Guides Travel Services Booking Form

Different Types of Breaks

Page Breaks can be used to mark the point at which one page ends and the next page begins, whilst Section Breaks start a new section on the next page. Both are visible in Print Layout View, Outline and Draft View.

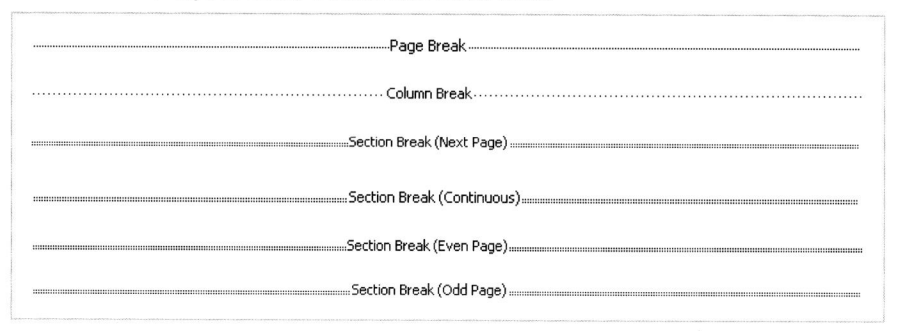

```
----------------------------------Page Break----------------------------------
.................................Column Break.................................
================Section Break (Next Page)================
================Section Break (Continuous)================
================Section Break (Even Page)================
================Section Break (Odd Page)================
```

Figure 64

Create a Section Break

1. Click Print Layout View positioned at the bottom right of the screen
2. Select the place in a document where a section break is required
3. Select Page Layout, Breaks to expand the menu
4. Choose **Next Page** – Insert a section break and start the new section on the next page.
5. Alternatively select ALT, I, B to display the Break dialog box

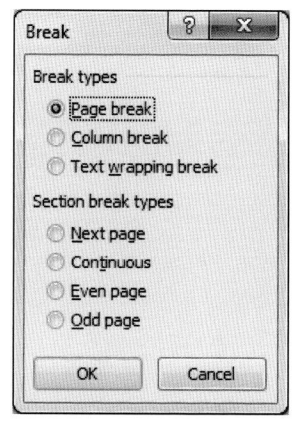

Break

Break types
- ● Page break
- ○ Column break
- ○ Text wrapping break

Section break types
- ○ Next page
- ○ Continuous
- ○ Even page
- ○ Odd page

OK   Cancel

Figure 65

6. Select <u>N</u>ext page, press OK

7. Choose **Orientation**, select **Landscape**
8. To create a section break on a new page, select **Breaks**
9. Select **Next Page** — Insert a section break and start the new section on the next page.
10. Change the orientation to **Portrait**
11. Select **File**, **Print**, use zoom to view the breaks
12. Alternatively press **CTRL** **F2**
13. Choose **ESC** on the keyboard to return to the document
14. Return to the top of Page 1
15. Select **Insert**, **Header**, **Edit Header**
16. Section 1 is displayed above the header box **Header -Section 1-**
17. Type Section 1 inside the header box, select **Next**
18. Choose **Link to Previous**
19. Type Section 2 inside the header box, click on **Next**
20. Select **Link to Previous**
21. Type Section 3 inside the header box
22. Click on **Go to Footer**, choose **Page Number**, **Bottom of Page**, to display the gallery

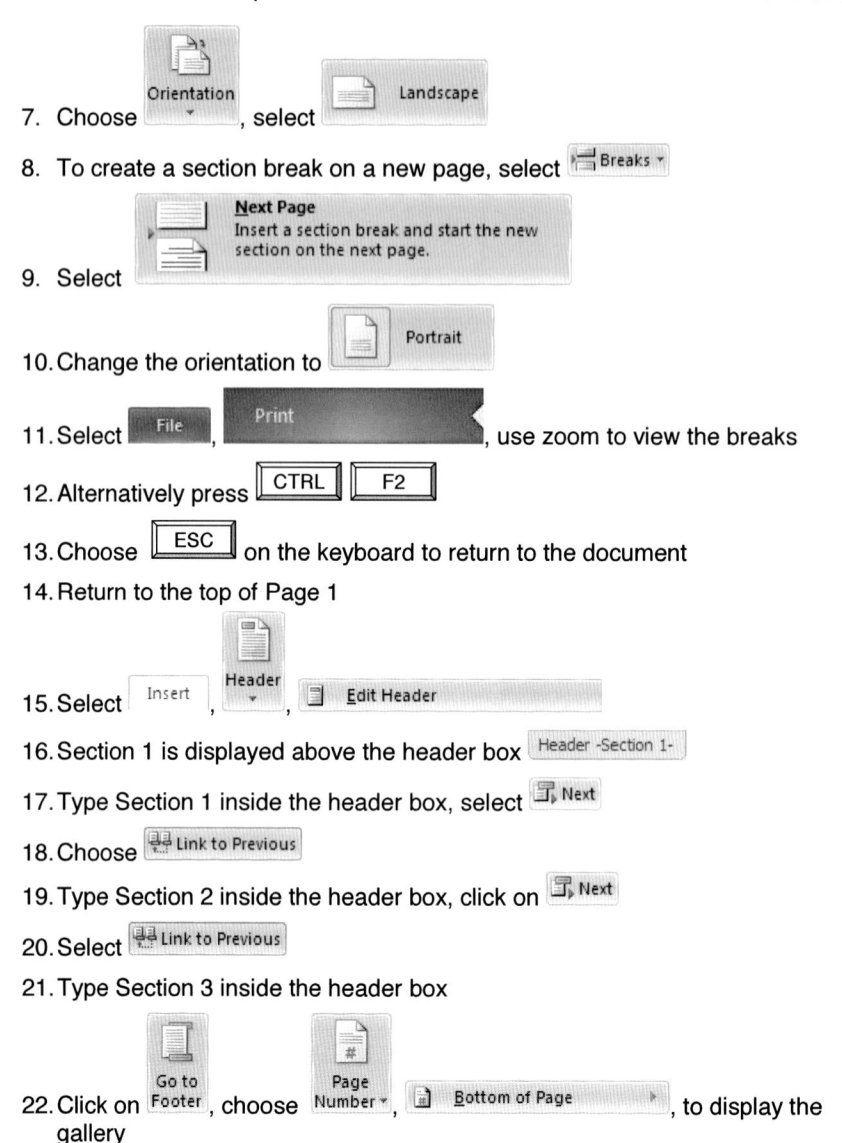

23. Using the downward arrows on the scroll bar ▼ select Page X of Y

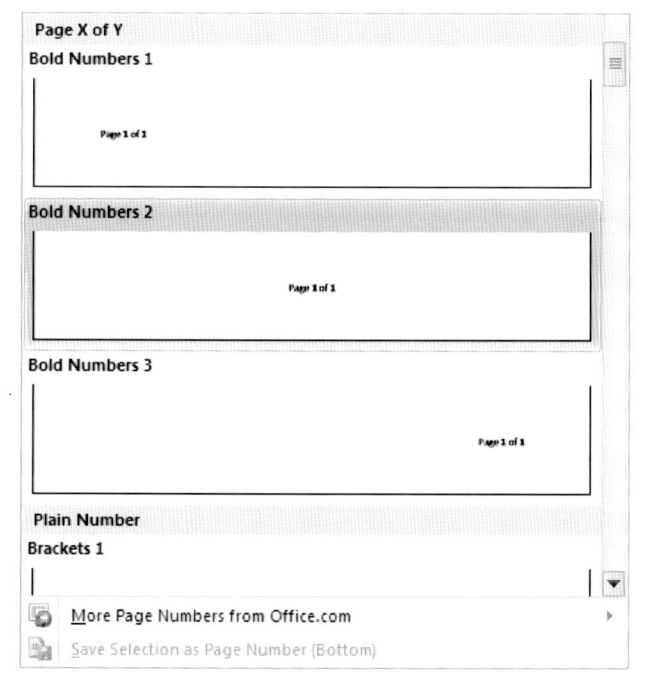

Figure 66

24. Choose the required option, page numbers appear at the foot of each page
25. Save the document as Working with Sections, preview the results

Delete a Page, Column or Section Break

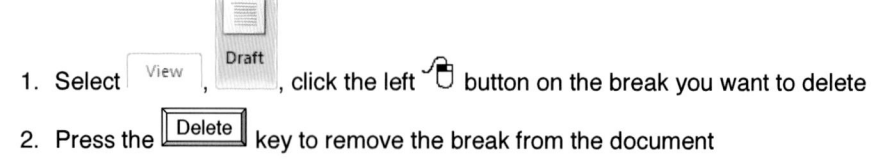

1. Select `View`, `Draft`, click the left 🖱 button on the break you want to delete
2. Press the `Delete` key to remove the break from the document
3. Alternatively press `ALT` `W` `E` to display the Draft View

Header and Footer: Moving between Sections

1. Select `Insert`, `Header`, `Edit Header`
2. Choose `Next` to display the next section
3. Click `Previous` to go back to the previous section
4. Select `Go to Footer` to switch from the header to the footer icon
5. Click `Go to Header` to return to the Header
6. Press `Close Header and Footer` to return to the document
7. Alternatively select Print Layout View
8. Double click with the left 🖱 button in the header or footer area
9. The `Header & Footer Tools` are displayed

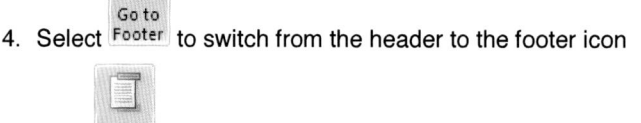

Exercise 7: - Creating a Header and Footer

1. Open Smart PC Guides Travel Services Booking Form
2. Select a style from the gallery
3. Centre align and type Smart PC Guides Booking Form in the Header
4. Go to the Footer and insert Page 1 of 1 from the gallery
5. Save the document

Identify the Tab Stop Marker

Setting tabs allows you to quickly create and align information in a document.

1. To display the ruler in Print Layout or Web Layout select `View`
2. Click with the left button on `☑ Ruler`
3. Alternatively select `ALT` `W` `R`

The default tab marker is set at 1.27cm

Figure 67

4. Select a new blank document
5. Click on the Show/Hide icon `¶` with the left button
6. Press `TAB` to move to the next default tab marker below the ruler
7. A tab stop is identified by a vertical grey line
8. The default tab is left aligned meaning the text appears from the left

Different Tab and Indent Icons

The following tab icons are displayed on the left hand side of the ruler.

Icons	Description of Icons in the Ruler
L	Left Tab
⊥	Centre Tab
⊣	Right Align Tab
⊥	Decimal Tab
ǀ	Bar Tab
▽	First Line Indent
▭	Hanging Indent

Figure 68

Setting Tabs from the Ruler

1. Move the mouse pointer over the left align icon `L`
2. Click with the left button, the icon changes with each click displaying the different tab options
3. Choose the left alignment tab `L`
4. Move the mouse pointer to 3cm on the ruler

5. Click with the left 🖱 button, the left tab is set
6. Set a right tab at 13cm and a decimal tab at 7.5cm
7. Insert a bar tab at 5cm and 10cm, the set tabs are shown below

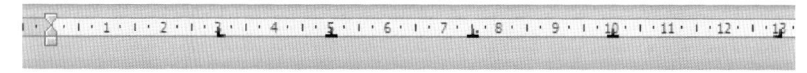

Figure 69

Removing Tabs from the Ruler

1. Move the mouse pointer 🖱 over the left align icon ⌐ in the ruler
2. Click and hold down the left 🖱 button
3. Drag the selected tab off the ruler, the tab is removed from the ruler

Setting Tabs from the Tab Dialog Box

1. Select `Home`, click the downward arrow from the Paragraph Grouping
2. The Paragraph dialog box appears

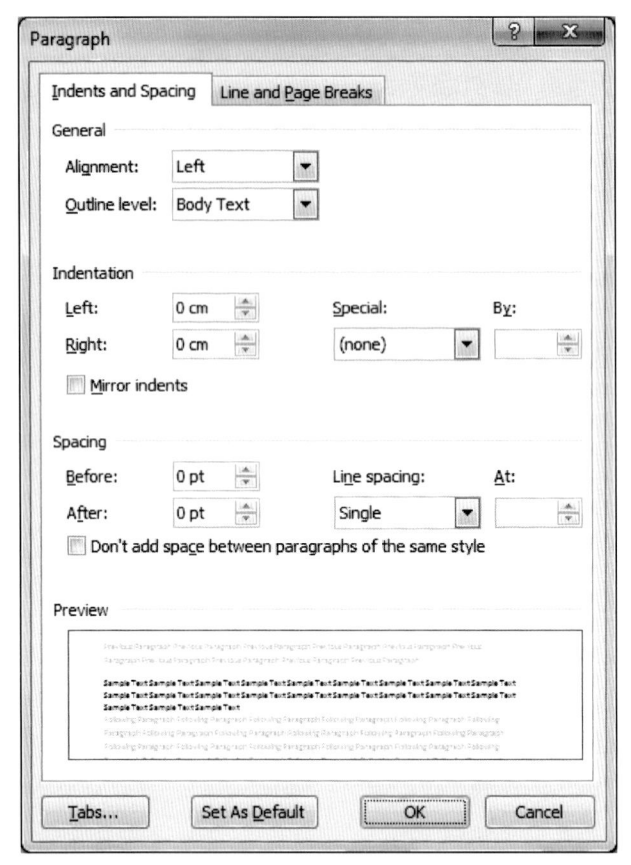

Figure 70

3. Select [Tabs...]
4. Alternatively press [ALT] [O] [T]
5. The Tabs dialog box appears

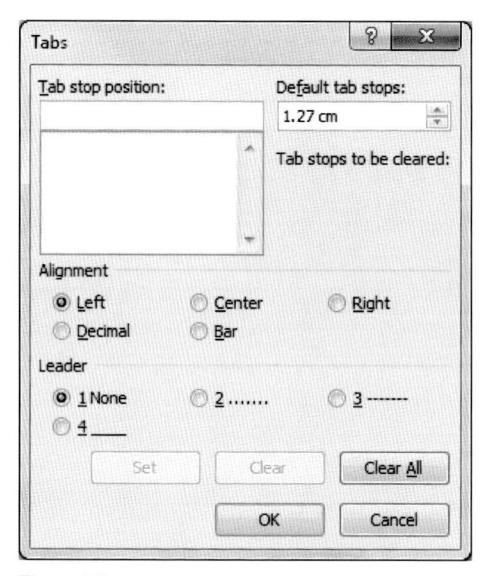

Figure 71

6. Select the Tab stop position
7. Type 3cm as the measurement for the tab stop
8. Select the Alignment Left, click [Set]
9. Repeat the above steps to set additional alignments
10. To remove an alignment click on the measurement
11. Click [Clear], select [OK]
12. Selecting [Clear All] reverts back to the default tab
13. To modify a tab stop, double click with the left button on the tab marker
14. The Tabs dialog box is displayed

Exercise 8: - Creating Tabs

Make/Model	Price	Location
BMW	£79,950.00	London
Range Rover	£59,000.00	Birmingham
Aston Martin	£92950.00	Newcastle
Ferrari	£107,950.00	Cardiff

1. Select a new blank document
2. Create a table with 3 columns and 1 row
3. Set a centre tab in column 1 at 2.5cm
4. Use `TAB` to move to column 2, press `F4`
5. Use `TAB` to move to column 3, press `F4`
6. The centre tabs in column 2 and 3 are created
7. Type the above headings in each column, press `Enter`
8. Click the left button after the heading named **Make/Model**, press `Enter`
9. Create the new tab stops for the remaining text
10. Set a left tab in column 1 at 1.5cm
11. Set a decimal tab in column 2 at 3cm
12. Set a left tab in column 3 at 1.9cm
13. Type in the text as shown above
14. Save the document as Working with Tabs

What are Styles?

A style is a series of formats that can be applied to individual characters or entire paragraphs that enhance the appearance of documents. A table of contents can be created using the styles formatted in the document.

Styles allows the user to change the format of documents, for example changing font, colour and typeface, alter alignments, indenting and line spacing, add number and bullet lists and create style headings and sub-headings. If styles are used in a document a Table of Contents can be generated automatically based upon the styles that have been formatted.

Displaying Styles in a Document

1. Select Draft View or Outline View
2. Choose **File**, **Options**, **Advanced**
3. Using the downward arrow select **Display**
4. Alternatively press **ALT** **F** **T** **A**
5. Scroll down to the Display area

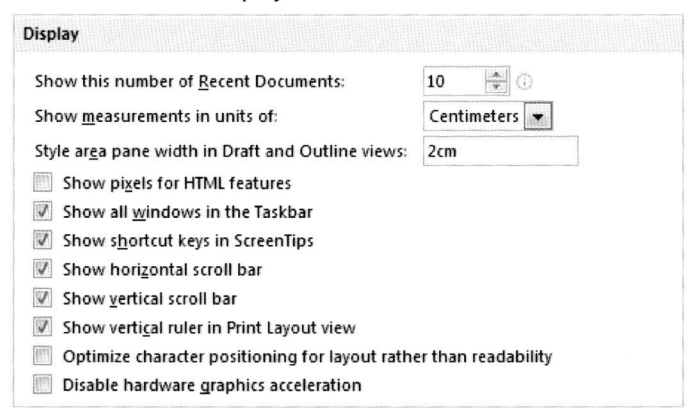

Figure 72

6. Change the measurement of the Style area pane width to 2cm
7. Select **OK**, the style area is displayed in the document

Normal ← Style area width

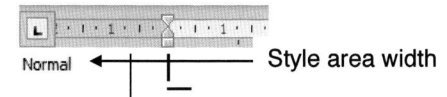

Figure 73

Working with Styles

1. Open a new document
2. Select `Home`
3. Click on the downward arrow from the Styles Grouping

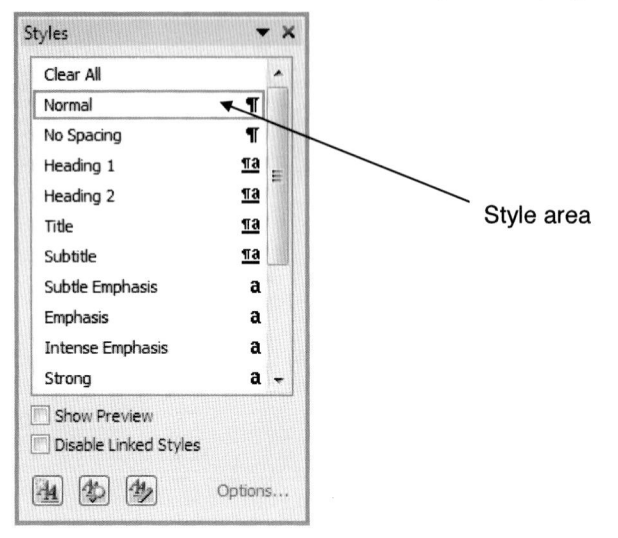

Figure 74

4. Select Heading 1, type Smart PC Guides
5. Select Heading 2, 3 and Normal Style to view the different styles
6. To clear formatting click on `Clear All`

Modifying a Style

1. Open a new blank document
2. Select `Home`
3. Click on the downward arrow from the Styles Grouping

`Heading 1`

Figure 75

4. Choose Heading 1, click with the right button on the downward arrow
5. Select `Modify...`
6. The Modify Style dialog box appears

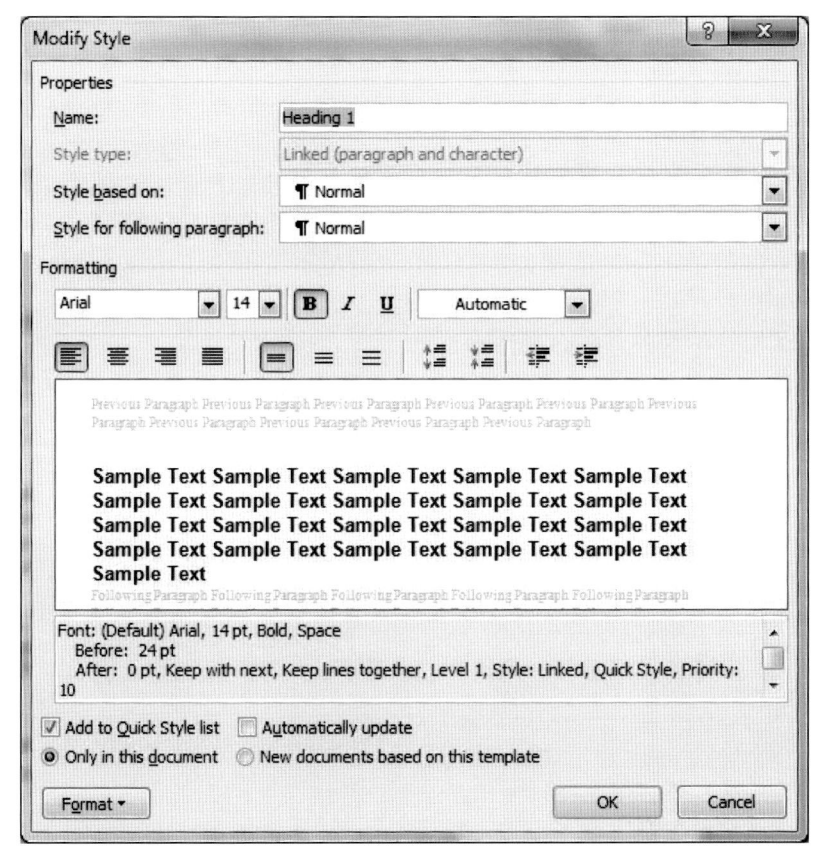

Figure 76

7. Change the formatting options as required, select [Format ▼]

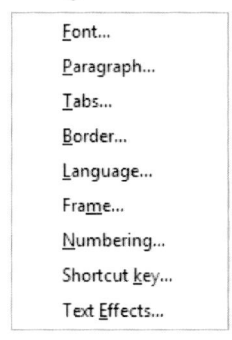

Figure 77

8. Click Font, change the colour, press [OK] twice
9. Ensure [✓ Show Preview] is selected in the style task pane area to display the modified style

Adding a Style to a Template

To add a style to a template, tick `New documents based on this template` in the Modify Style dialog box.

Automatic Update Feature

Use the automatic update feature with extreme care. Any changes made to the alignment of a document using the `Automatically update` option changes all the text.

Creating a New Style

1. Click on a new blank document
2. Select `Home`, click on the downward arrow from the Styles Grouping
3. The Styles window is displayed
4. Choose Heading Style 1 from the Styles Gallery
5. Select the New Style icon
6. The Create New Style from Formatting dialog box appears

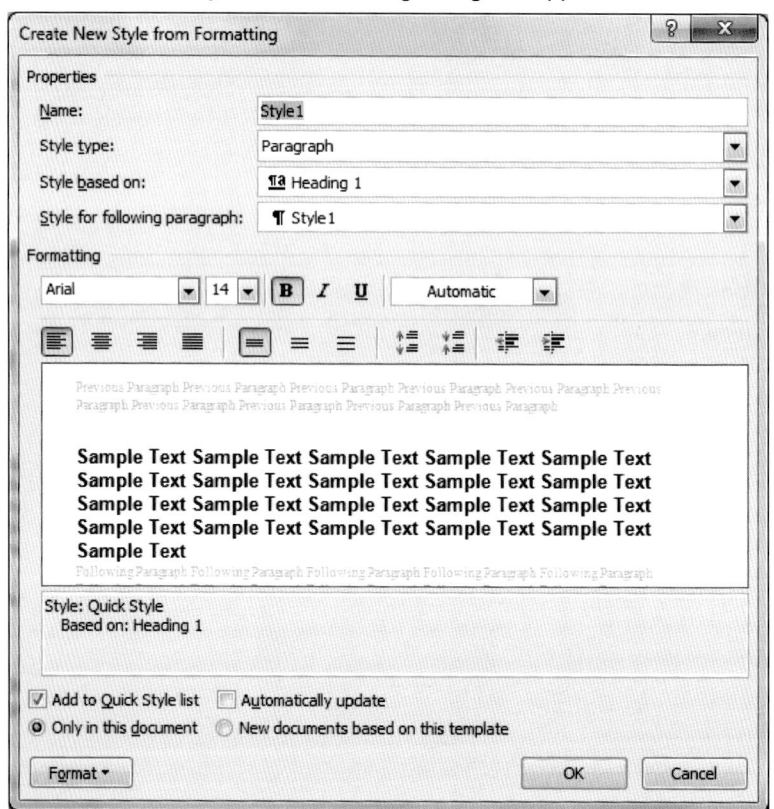

Figure 78

7. Select **N**ame, type `Smart PC Guides New Style`
8. Click `Format ▼`, modify the style to your requirements
9. Click `OK`
10. The style appears in the Styles area `Smart PC Guides New Style ▼`

Assign a Shortcut Key to a Style

1. Choose Smart PC Guides New Style
2. Select `▲ Modify...`
3. The Modify Style dialog box appears

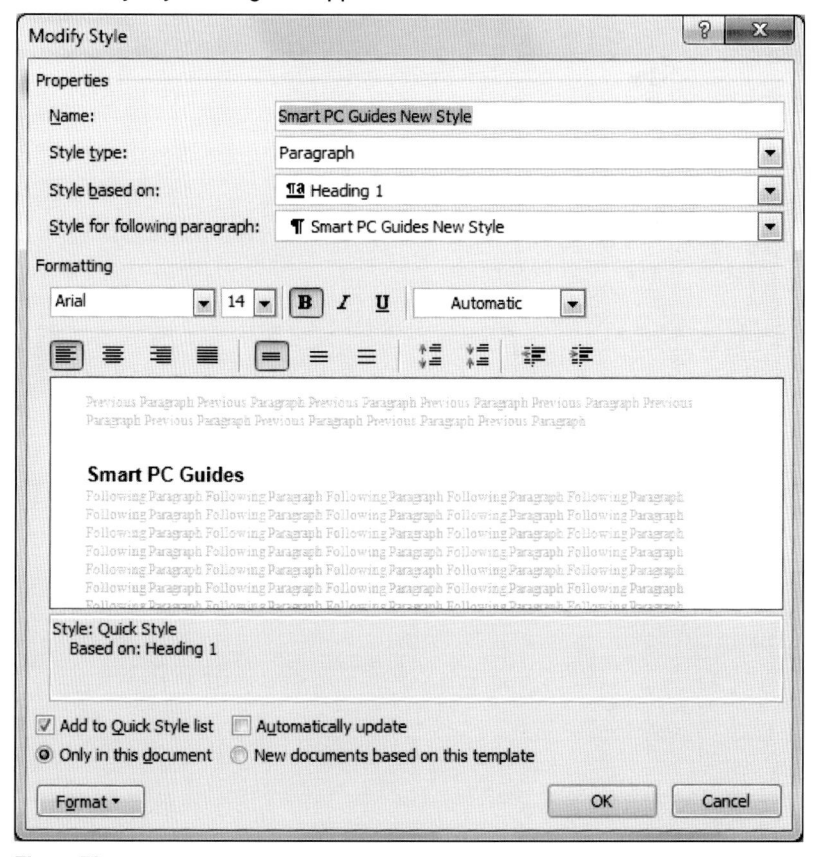

Figure 79

4. Click with the left 🖱 button on `Format ▼`

5. Select `Shortcut key...`, the Customise Keyboard dialog box appears

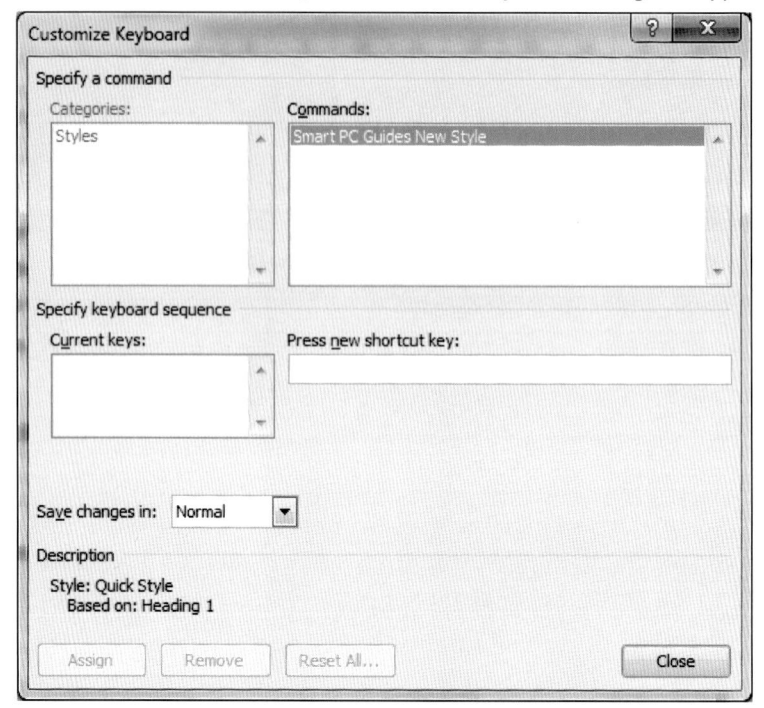

Figure 80

6. Smart PC Guides New Style appears in the `Commands:` box
7. Go to `Press new shortcut key:`
8. Hold down the `ALT` key, press `5`
9. Click `Assign`, choose `Close`
10. Click with the left 🖱 button in the `◉ New documents based on this template` dialog box
11. Select `OK`

Deleting a Style from a Template

1. Select `Home`, click on the downward arrow from the Styles Grouping
2. Select Smart PC Guides New Style
3. Choose the Manage Styles icon, the Manage Styles dialog box appears

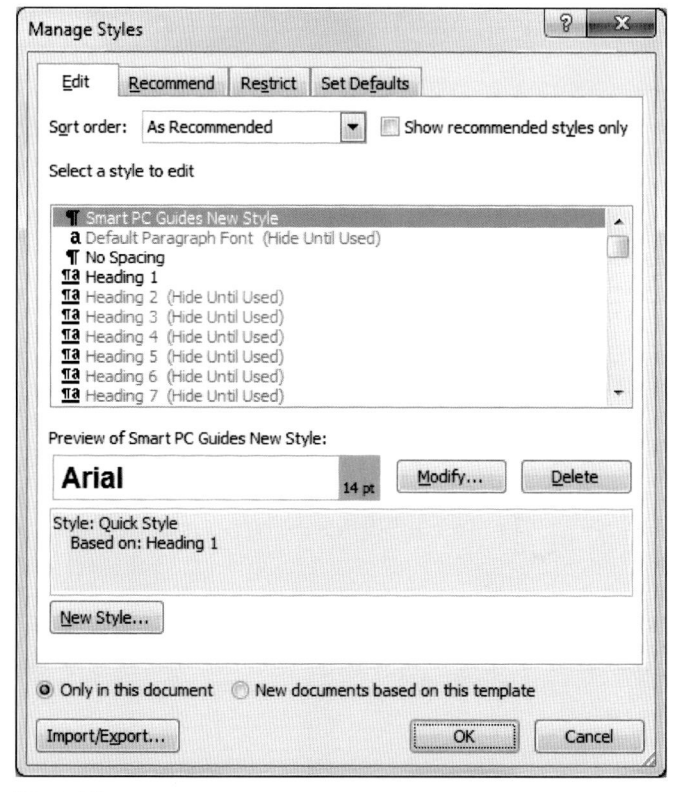

Figure 81

4. To delete the style from the template select `Import/Export...`
5. The Organiser dialog box appears

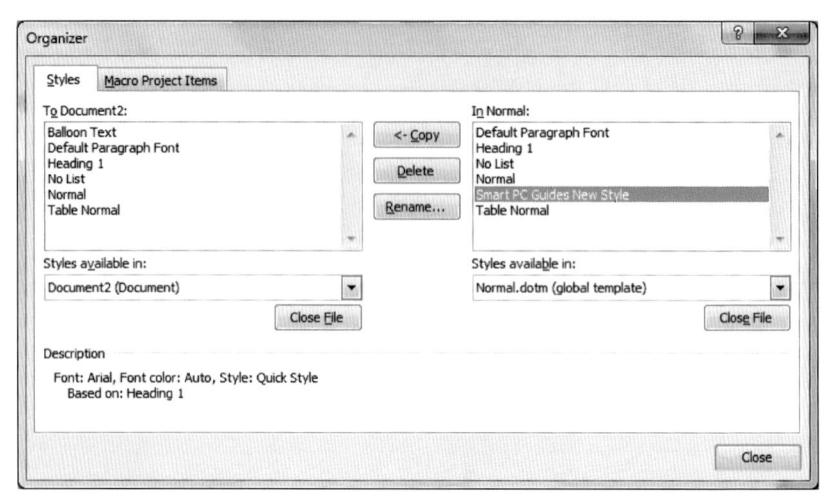

Figure 82

6. Go to **In** Normal area, select Smart PC Guides New Style
7. Press `Delete`

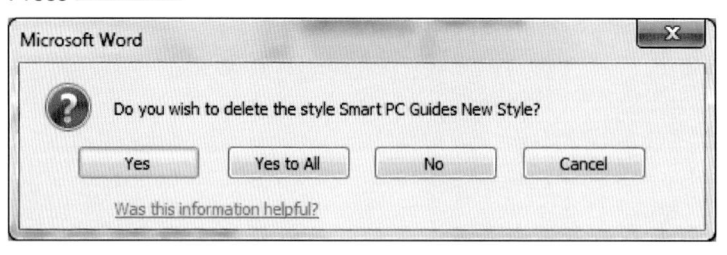

Figure 83

8. Press `Yes to All` to delete the style from the Normal.dotm (global template)
9. Click `Close`
10. Open a new document
11. Press `ALT` `CTRL` `SHIFT` `S` to display the Styles window
12. Smart PC Guides New Style has been deleted
13. Switch to Print Layout View

Exercise 9: - Creating a Document using Styles

1. Open a new blank document
2. On Page 1 select Heading Style 1, type Monday
3. Press `Enter`, select Heading Style 2, type Briefing at 10.00
4. On Page 2 select Heading Style 1, type Tuesday
5. Press `Enter`, select Heading Style 2, type Performance Review at 15.00
6. On Page 3 select Heading Style 1, type Wednesday
7. Press `Enter`, select Heading Style 3, type Progress Meeting 09.30
8. On Page 4 select Heading Style 1, type Thursday
9. Press `Enter`, select Heading Style 2, type Staff Appraisal at 14.15
10. On Page 5 select Heading Style 1, type Friday
11. Press `Enter`, select Heading Style 3, type Company Car New Criteria
12. Preview the document, check the newly created styles on each page
13. Save the document as Working with Styles
14. Close the document

Bookmarks

Setting a bookmark allows text to be found easily for future reference.

Adding a Bookmark

1. Click with the left 🖱 button in a document a bookmark is to be added
2. Select **Insert**, **Bookmark** from the Links Grouping
3. Type the bookmark name

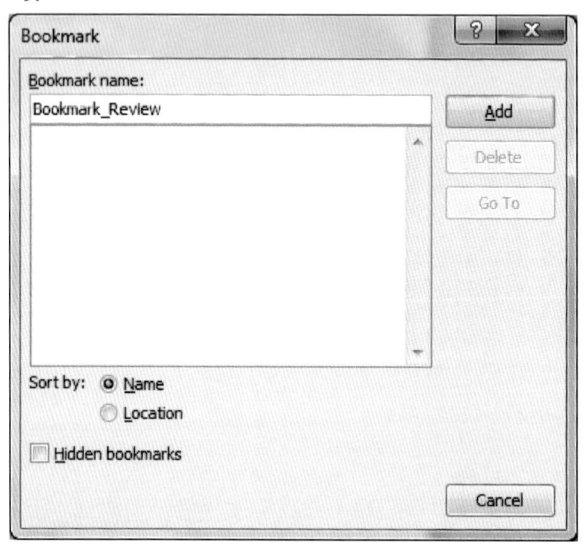

Figure 84

4. Click **Add**
5. Alternatively **ALT** **N** **K** displays the Bookmark dialog box

Note: The underscore character can be used to separate words when defining a name.

Locating a Bookmark

1. Select `Insert`, `Bookmark`, select the bookmark name

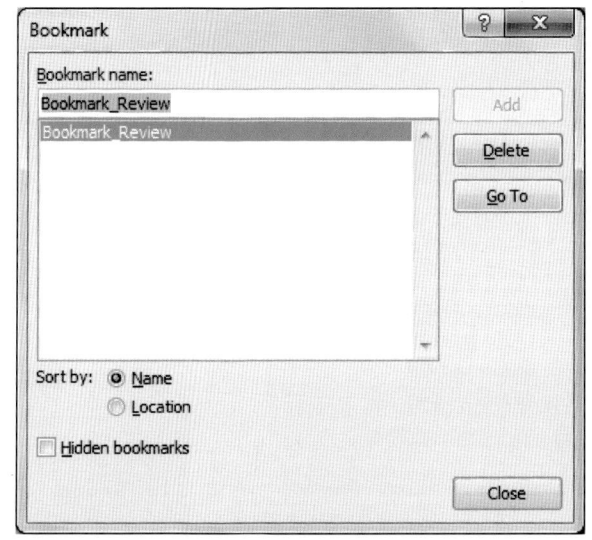

Figure 85

2. Click `Go To`, choose `Close`
3. Alternatively `F5` displays the **G**o To dialog box

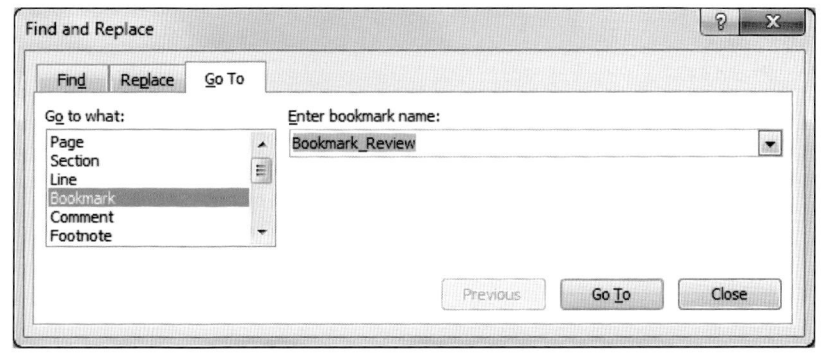

Figure 86

4. Click with the left button on the word Bookmark
5. Ensure the bookmark name **Bookmark_Review** is selected
6. Select `Go To`, click `Close`

Deleting a Bookmark

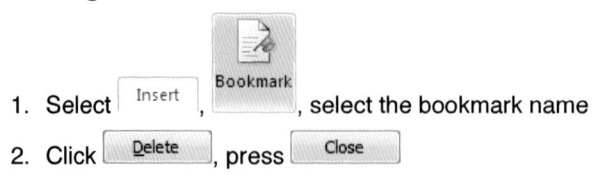

1. Select `Insert`, `Bookmark`, select the bookmark name
2. Click `Delete`, press `Close`

Creating a Table of Contents

A Table of Contents is a structured list of a document's content. If the document was constructed using styles, a Table of Contents can be generated automatically.

1. Open the document Working with Styles
2. Hold down the `CTRL` and `HOME` keys, go to page 1
3. Select Draft View and create a page break
4. Click in the new page, press `Enter`
5. Ensure the cursor is at the top of the new page
6. Choose Normal Style
7. Using the Formatting Grouping change the font to Arial, size 14, Bold

Figure 87

8. Centre align and type out Table of Contents on the first page
9. Press `Enter`, select, Align Left
10. Select `References`, `Table of Contents`, `Insert Table of Contents...`
11. `ALT` `S` `T` `I` displays the Table of Contents dialog box

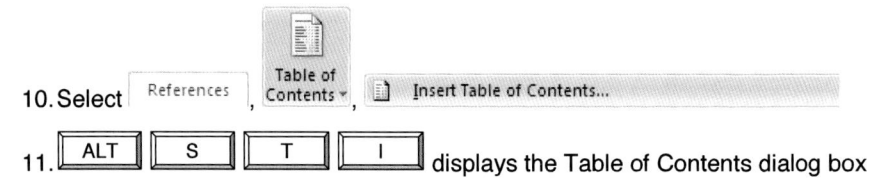

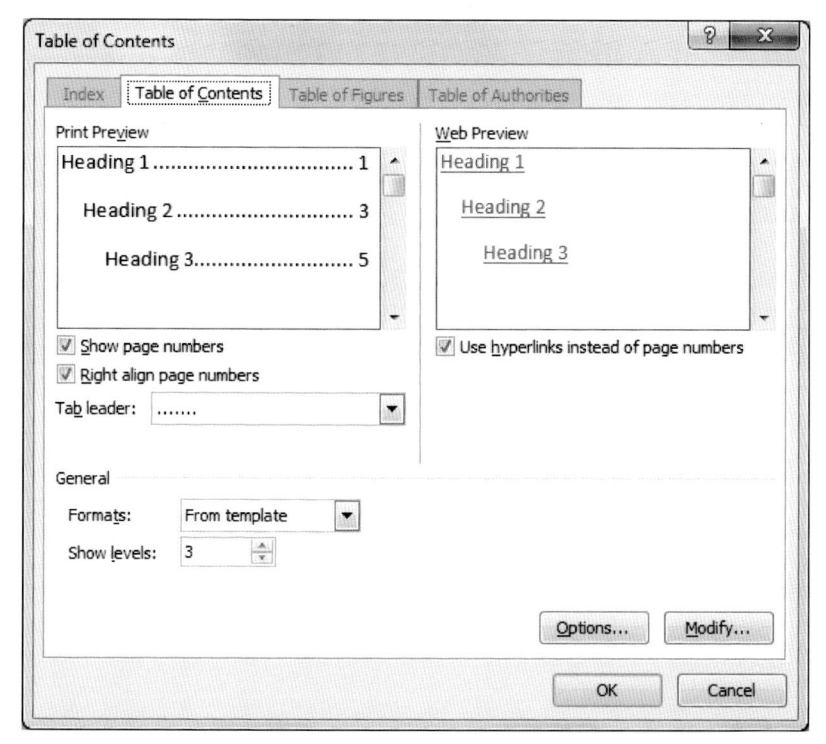

Figure 88

12. Print Pre**v**iew displays the layout of the Table of Contents
13. Select [OK] the Table of Contents appears in the document
14. Switch to Print Layout View
15. Save the document

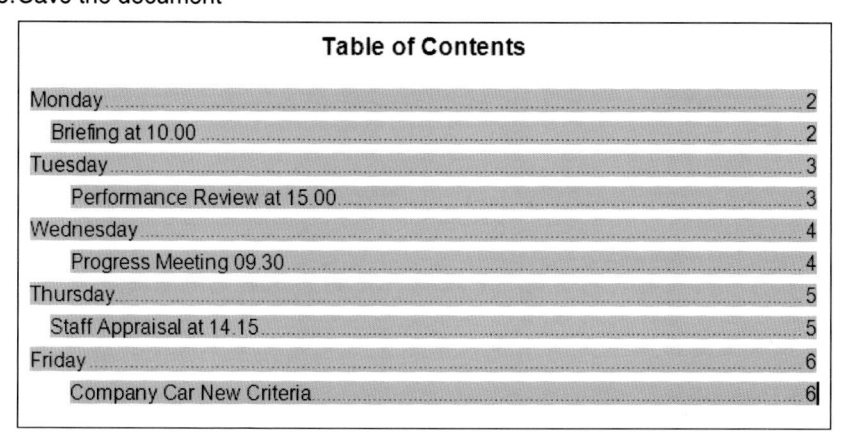

Table of Contents	
Monday	2
Briefing at 10.00	2
Tuesday	3
Performance Review at 15.00	3
Wednesday	4
Progress Meeting 09.30	4
Thursday	5
Staff Appraisal at 14.15	5
Friday	6
Company Car New Criteria	6

Figure 89

Exercise 10: - Updating a Table of Contents

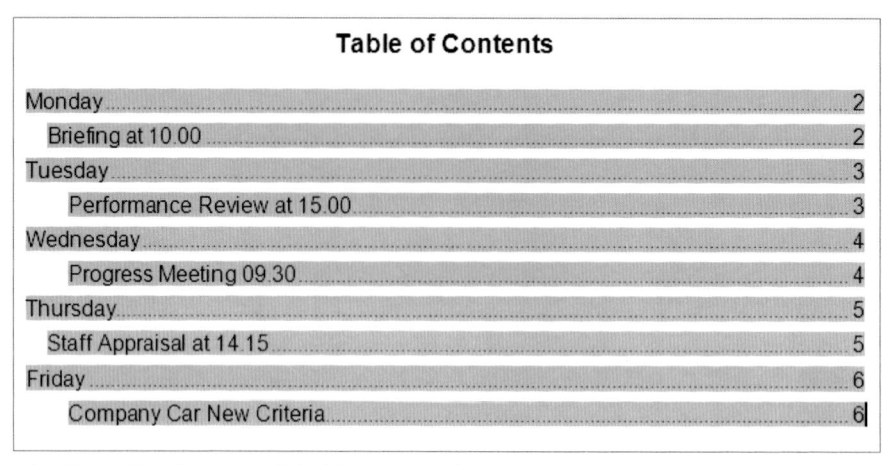

Table of Contents	
Monday	2
Briefing at 10.00	2
Tuesday	3
Performance Review at 15.00	3
Wednesday	4
Progress Meeting 09.30	4
Thursday	5
Staff Appraisal at 14.15	5
Friday	6
Company Car New Criteria	6

1. Open the document Working with Styles
2. Select `View`, `Outline`
3. Hold down `CTRL`, move the mouse pointer over page 2
4. Click on the page number, the cursor appears on page 2
5. Change Briefing at 10:00 to Heading Style 3
6. Select `References`, click `Update Table`
7. Select Update **e**ntire table

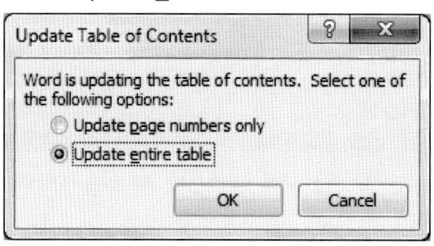

   Update Table of Contents
   Word is updating the table of contents. Select one of the following options:
   ○ Update page numbers only
   ● Update entire table
   [OK] [Cancel]

8. Choose `OK`
9. Change Company Car New Criteria to Heading Style 2, click `Update Table`
10. Update the entire table, view the updated Table of Contents
11. Hold down `CTRL`, move the mouse pointer over page 2
12. The mouse pointer changes to 👆
13. Click on the page number, page 2 is displayed, save the document

Indexes

Long documents normally have a reference guide at the back of the document known as an index. The index identifies keywords and subjects frequently used in a document.

Creating an Index

1. Open the document Working with Styles
2. Select `References`, `Insert Index`
3. The Index dialog box appears

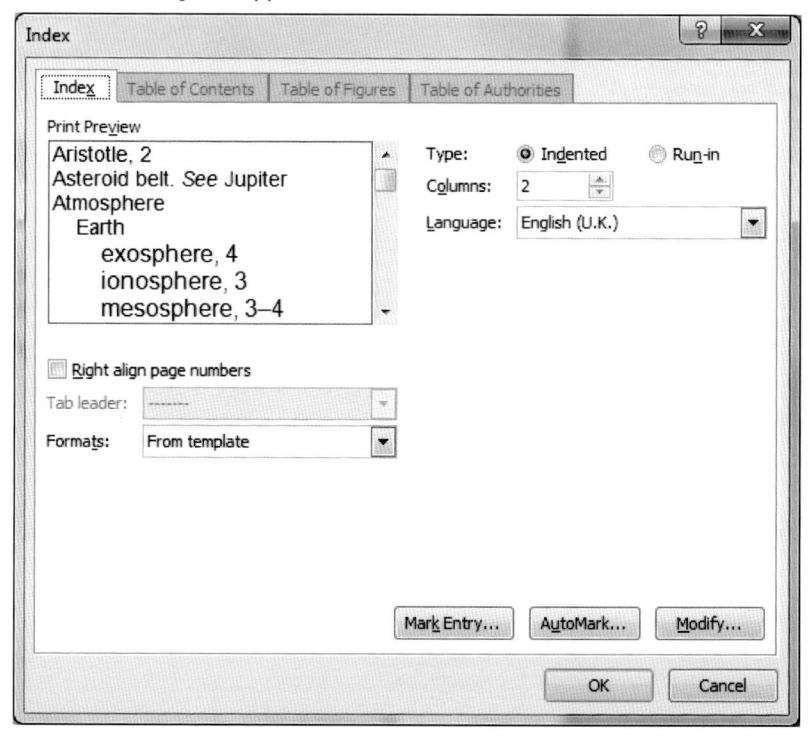

Figure 90

4. Select `Type:` `Indented` choose `Columns: 1`
5. Change the dialog as below

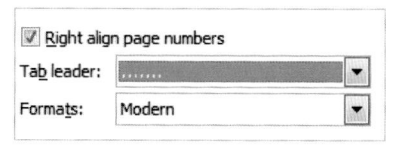

Figure 91

6. Click Mark Entry...

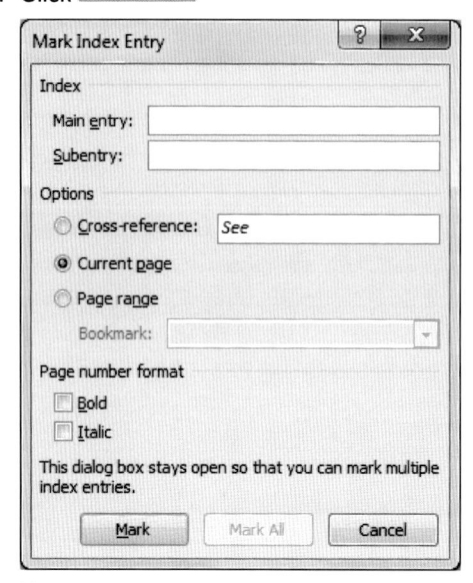

Figure 92

7. Create Main entries and Subentries from the table below

Select	In Mark Index Type	Click
Main entry	Monday	Mark
Subentry	Briefing	
Main entry	Briefing	Mark
Subentry	Monday	
Main entry	Tuesday	Mark
Subentry	Performance	
Main entry	Performance	Mark
Subentry	Review	
Main entry	Review	Mark
Subentry	Tuesday	

Figure 93

8. Create Main entry and Subentries for Wednesday to Friday

9. Click Close, go to the end of the document and create a new page

10. Select References, Insert Index, click Close

A

Appraisal
  Thursday --5

B

Briefing
  Monday --2

C

Company Car
  Friday --6

F

Friday
  Company Car --6

M

Monday
  Briefing --2

P

Performance
  Review --3
  Tuesday ---3
Progress
  Wednesday ---4

R

Review
  Performance --3

T

Thursday
  Appraisal ---5
Tuesday
  Performance --3

W

Wednesday
  Progress --4

Figure 94

Bibliography, Citations and Plagiarism

The word bibliographia was first used by Greek writers to mean the copying of books by hand, the modern meaning of a bibliography is the description of books or a list of sources, usually placed at the end of a document that the writer has consulted or cited in creating a document. Microsoft Word generates a bibliography based on the source information that the writer has provided for the document, sometimes called a reference list. Each time a new source is created, the source information is saved on your computer, so that the reader of the document can find and use any source created.

A citation is the information needed to locate the book to help readers of the document to go to the information used. Citation formats may vary but an entry for a book in a bibliography usually contains the author(s) name, the title of the book, the publisher and the date of the publication. The bibliography may be arranged by author, topic or some other scheme.

Plagiarism is copying another author's work or borrowing someone else's original ideas and passing them off as their own. To avoid plagiarism the writer of the document should always acknowledge the source of their research; it also shows the amount of research done in creating the document. Citations should be used whenever quotes or paraphrases are used, when someone else's expressed idea is used, when specific reference to the work of another is used, or whenever someone else's work has been critical in developing the writers own ideas.

Add a Citation and Source to a Document

When you add a new citation to a document, a new source will also be created that will appear in the bibliography.

1. Open a new document
2. Type the following passage, ensure quotation marks are used at the beginning and end of the text

"You either love it or hate it! Whatever you feel gardening is the perfect way to wheel away the stresses of the day. Once you have grasped how a plant works you are in a position to bend it to your will. There are not many plants in the garden that can be left entirely to their own devices and the right time to do a job in the garden is when you have the time to do it properly.

Pruning is the removal of stems, branches or roots of a tree or shrub in order to alter the shape of the plant, to increase vigour or remove dead or damaged parts. It also helps to improve the quality and quantity of flowers and fruits. Dead heading is one sort of summer pruning we can do that not only keeps the plant tidy but it encourages a new growth of flowers within days."

3. Choose the References Tab

Figure 95

4. In the Citations and Bibliography Grouping
5. Click with the left 🖱 button in the Style area on the downward arrow
6. Choose the style GB7714 `Style: GB7714` to be used in the document for the citation and source
7. Click at the end of the sentence or phrase that requires a citation
8. Click with the left 🖱 button on `Insert Citation`, select `Add New Source...`
9. The Create Source dialog box appears

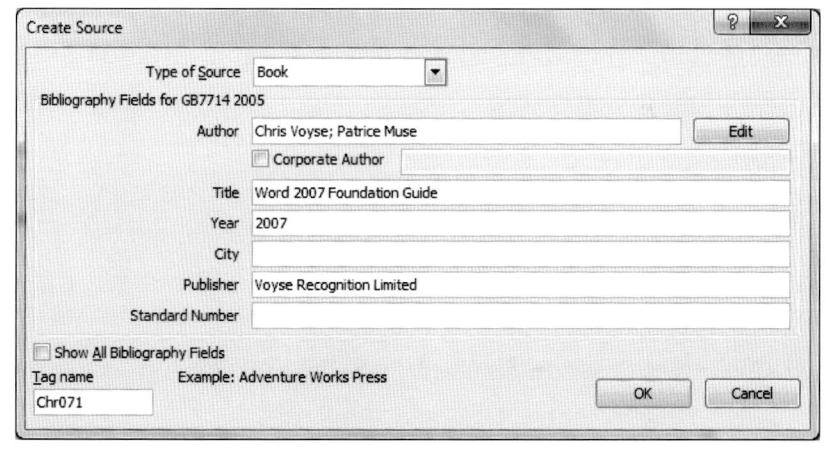

Figure 96

10. Complete the bibliography information for the source as above
11. Click with the left 🖱 button on `Show All Bibliography Fields`
12. This displays more fields to add more information about a source if required
13. In the Pages field type 13, a **T**ag name has been created, click `OK`

14. The citation will appear at the end of the text

> "You either love it or hate it! Whatever you feel gardening is the perfect way to wheel away the stresses of the day. Once you have grasped how a plant works you are in a position to bend it to your will. There are not many plants in the garden that can be left entirely to their own devices and the right time to do a job in the garden is when you have the time to do it properly.
>
> Pruning is the removal of stems, branches or roots of a tree or shrub in order to alter the shape of the plant, to increase vigour or remove dead or damaged parts. It also helps to improve the quality and quantity of flowers and fruits. Dead heading is one sort of summer pruning we can do that not only keeps the plant tidy but it encourages a new growth of flowers within days." (Voyse, et al., 2007)

Add a Bibliography at the End of a Document

1. Place the cursor at the end of the document
2. Select **Bibliography** from the References Tab

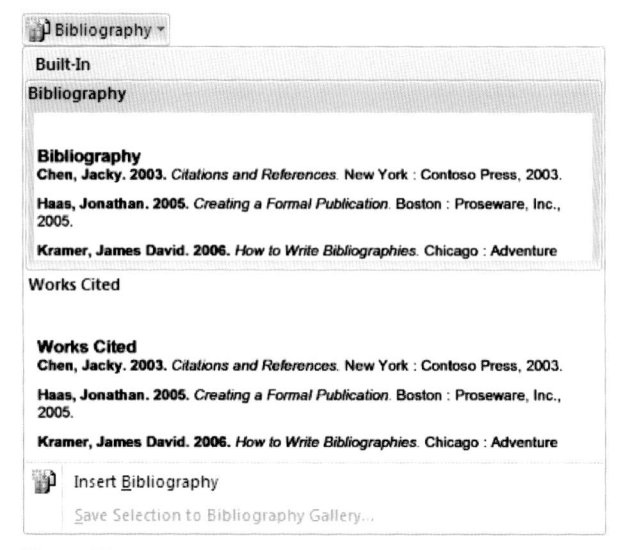

Figure 97

3. Choose the option Bibliography

Figure 98

4. The Bibliography appears at the end of the document

> **Bibliography**
> **Voyse, Chris and Muse, Patrice. 2007.** *Word 2007 Foundation Guide.* s.l. : Voyse Recognition Limited, 2007. p. 13.

Figure 99

5. Highlight the text to format to the required font size and style
6. Alternatively select **Bibliography** from the References Tab
7. Click on the downward pointing arrow, choose **Insert Bibliography**
8. Save the document as Adding a Bibliography

Edit a Citation or Source

1. Select **Manage Sources** from the **References** Tab
2. The Source Manager dialog box appears

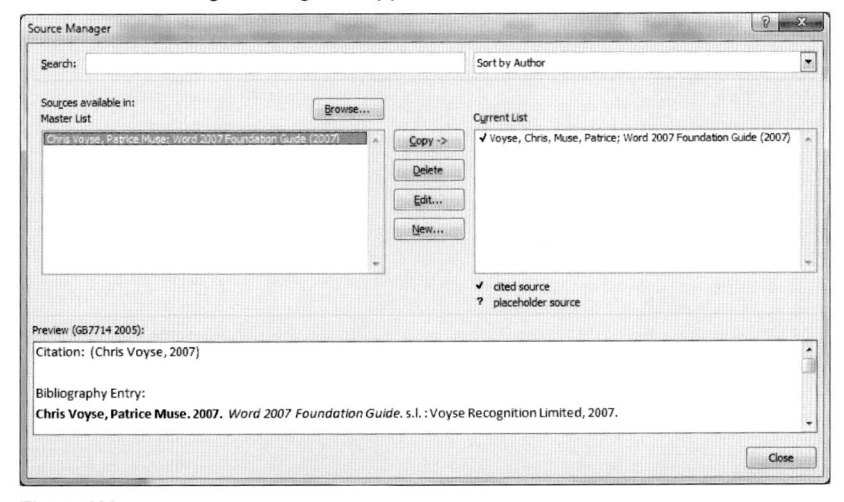

Figure 100

3. To Edit a source select **Edit...**

4. The Edit Source dialog box appears

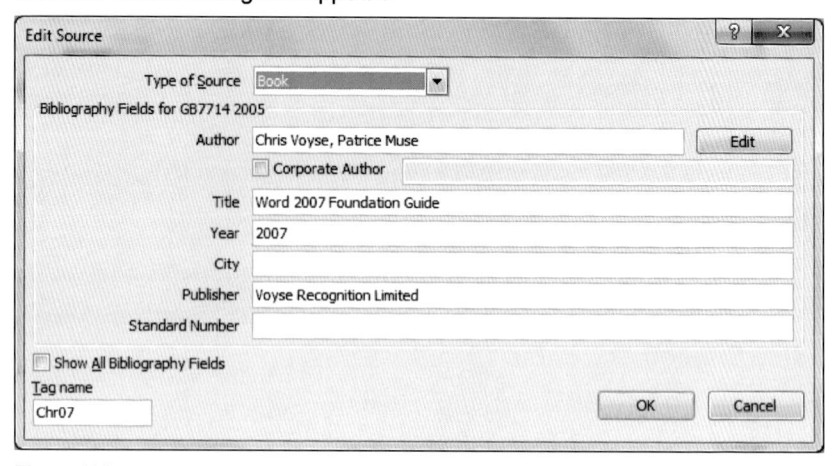

Figure 101

5. Make the necessary changes
6. Press [OK]
7. The following prompt appears

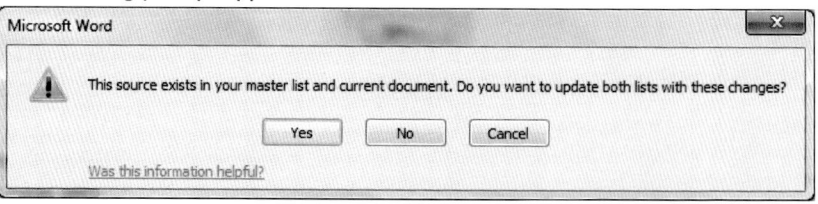

Figure 102

8. Press `Yes`, select `Close`

Delete a Citation or Source

1. To delete a source, select `Manage Sources` from the References Tab
2. The Source Manager dialog box appears

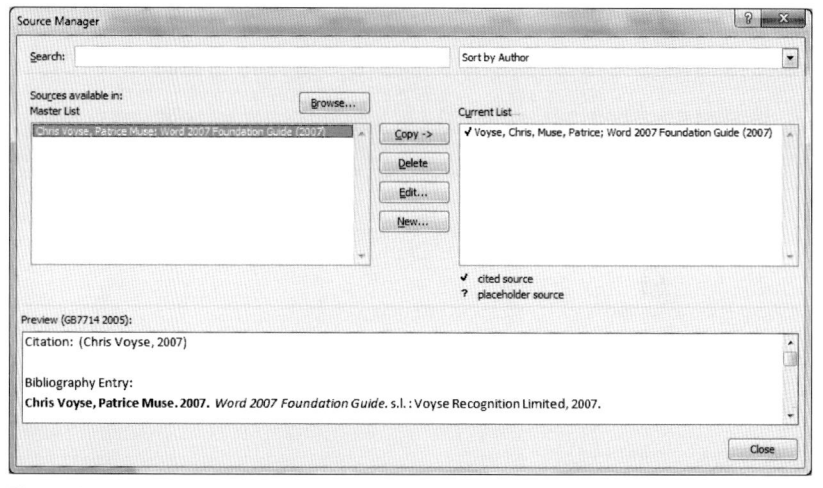

Figure 103

3. Click on the source(s) to be deleted
4. The Master List shows all sources used in previous documents
5. The Current List shows all sources used in the opened document
6. Select `Delete`, the source is deleted from the Source Manager
7. Press `Close`
8. Click on the Bibliography at the end of the document
9. Select `Update Citations and Bibliography`

Bibliography
Chris Voyse, Patrice Muse. *Word 2007 Foundation Guide*. s.l. : Voyse Recognition Limited.

Figure 104

10. The citation or source is removed

Exercise 11: - Add a Bibliography

1. Create a new document
2. Type the following text in the document
3. "The AutoSummarise feature gives a score to each sentence based on the number of words most frequently used in a sentence. Word automatically summarises these key points to create a summary for others to read. The user can then select how much detail you wish to use in the summary."
4. Ensure quotation marks are used at the beginning and end of the text
5. Create the following citation
    a. Type of Source: Book
    b. Author(s): Chris Voyse; Patrice Muse
    c. Title: Word 2007 Foundation to Expert Guide
    d. Year: 2007
    e. Publisher: Voyse Recognition Limited
    f. Pages: 89
6. Add the citation to the end of the text
7. Update the bibliography at the end of the document
8. Save the document

Reviewing a Document using Track Changes

Track Changes allows the user to make and view changes and comments made to a document.

How to use Track Changes

1. Open the document that requires changes to be made, select `Review`
2. Click on the downward arrow of the Track Changes icon `Track Changes`
3. Choose `Track Changes`
4. Highlight the text in the document that requires a change
5. Press `Delete`
6. The deleted text is displayed in the document highlighted in red with a strikethrough
7. New text inserted is highlighted and underlined
8. Alternatively any changes made can be viewed in the margin
9. Select `Show Markup`, `Balloons`, click on the downward pointing arrow to expand the menu
10. Select `Show Revisions in Balloons`

Figure 105

11. Click on `Reviewing Pane` in the Tracking Grouping
12. Select `Reviewing Pane Vertical...` to view changes made using the Reviewing Pane Vertically

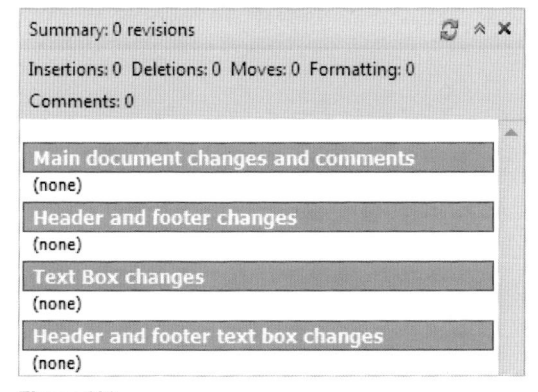

Figure 106

13. Or select [Reviewing Pane Horizontal...] to view changes made using the Reviewing Pane Horizontally

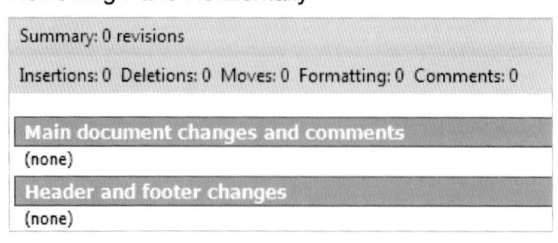

Figure 107

14. To choose how to see changes in the document

15. Select [Final: Show Markup], click on the downward arrow to expand the menu

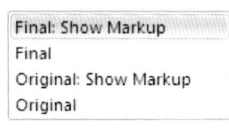

Figure 108

16. Select the required option

Comments

Inserting a Comment

1. Click where the comment is to appear in the document
2. Select [Review], [New Comment]
3. Type the required text in the balloon
4. The comment appears on the right-hand side of the document

Comment [CV1]: PM to review by September

Figure 109

Editing a Comment

1. Select the comment to be edited
2. Click in the comment box on the right-hand side of the document
3. Edit the comment as required

Viewing Comments

1. Select the comment to be viewed
2. Choose **Previous** to see the previous comment in the document
3. Select **Next** to see the next comment in the document

Deleting a Comment

1. Select the comment to be deleted
2. Click in the balloon on the right hand side of the document
3. Select **Delete**
4. To delete all the comments in a document
5. Click on the downward arrow, choose **Delete All Comments in Document**

Compare and Combine Multiple Copies

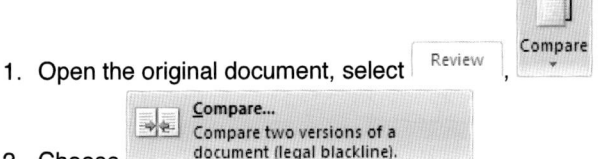

1. Open the original document, select **Review**, **Compare**
2. Choose **Compare... Compare two versions of a document (legal blackline).**
3. The Compare Documents dialog box appears

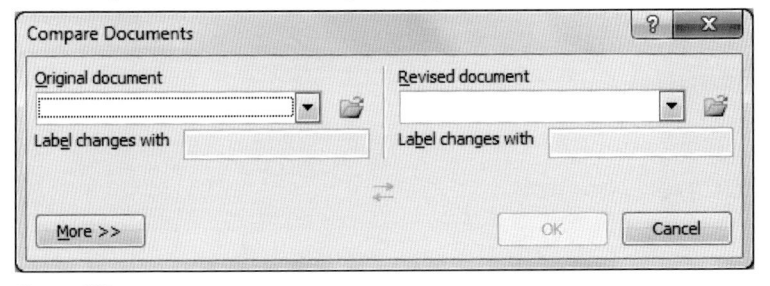

Figure 110

4. Click on the downward pointing arrow of the **O**riginal document box
5. Select and open the original document
6. Select and open the **R**evised document

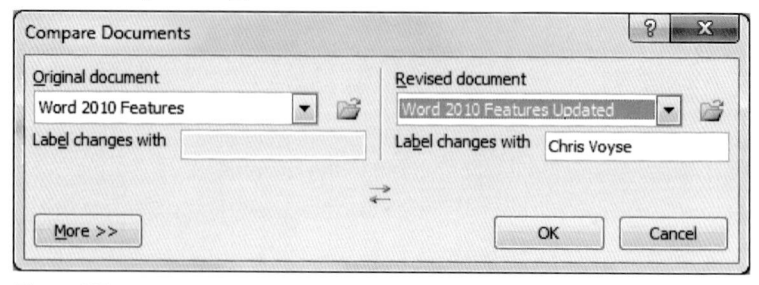

Figure 111

7. The More >> icon in the Compare Documents dialog box enables the user to select the comparison settings and show changes to the documents
8. Select << Less to reduce the size of the Compare Documents dialog box
9. Choose OK

Note: Changes made in the More options automatically become the default options the next time the compare documents is used.

10. The documents appear on screen

Original Document (Word 2010 Features)

Word 2010 Features

Revised Document (Word 2010 Features)

Word 2010 Features

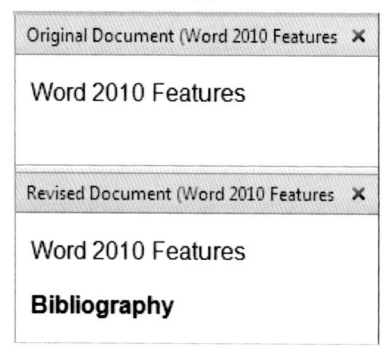

Bibliography

Figure 112

11. To merge the documents
12. Select Compare , Combine... Combine revisions from multiple authors into a single document.

13. The Combine Documents dialog box appears

Figure 113

14. Open the original document and the revised document, press OK

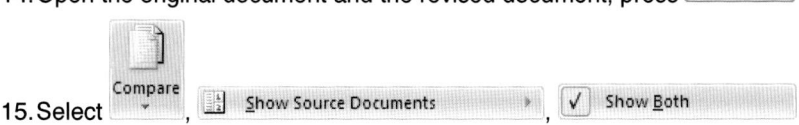

15. Select Compare, Show Source Documents, ✓ Show Both

16. The following prompt appears if formatting changes have been applied

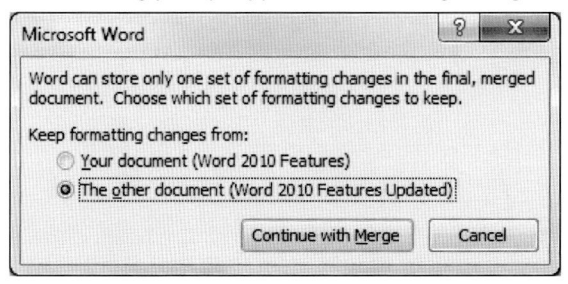

Figure 114

17. Select the required option, choose Continue with Merge

18. The combined document appears on screen

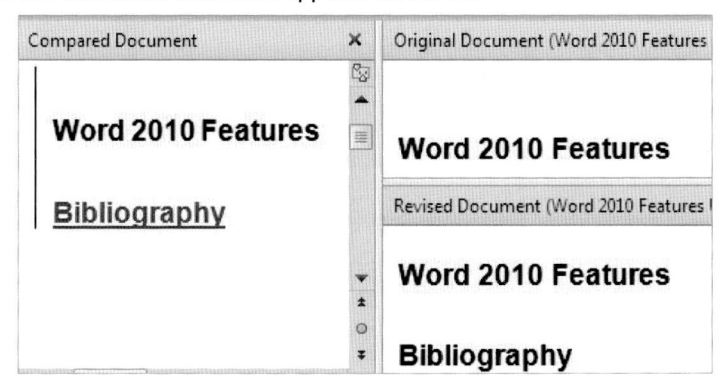

Figure 115

Mail Merge

Mail Merge is a quick way of merging information from one document into another allowing you to send personalised letters to groups of people or individuals by creating a main letter and a list of addresses that Word merges automatically. In order to do this two documents are needed, a Main document and a Data document.

Creating Letters using Mail Merge

1. Open a new document
2. Select **Mailings**, **Start Mail Merge**, **Step by Step Mail Merge Wizard...**

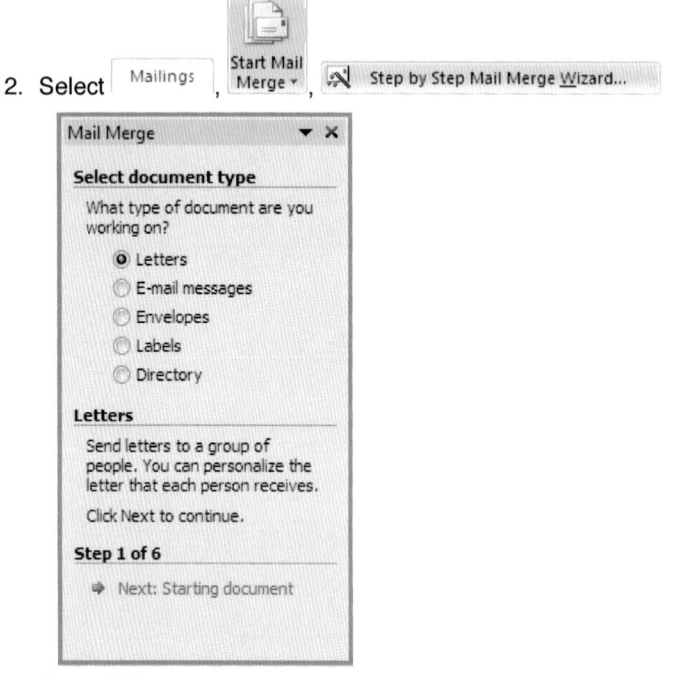

Figure 116

3. Select Letters from the document type
4. Click on Next: Starting Document to move to Step 2

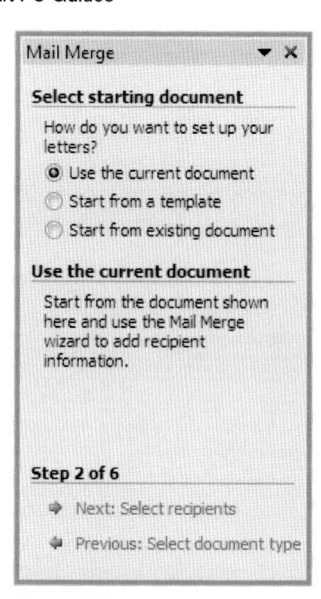

Figure 117

5. Select Use the current document
6. Click on Next: Select recipients to move to Step 3

Figure 118

7. Choose Type a new list, click Create...

8. The New Address List dialog box appears

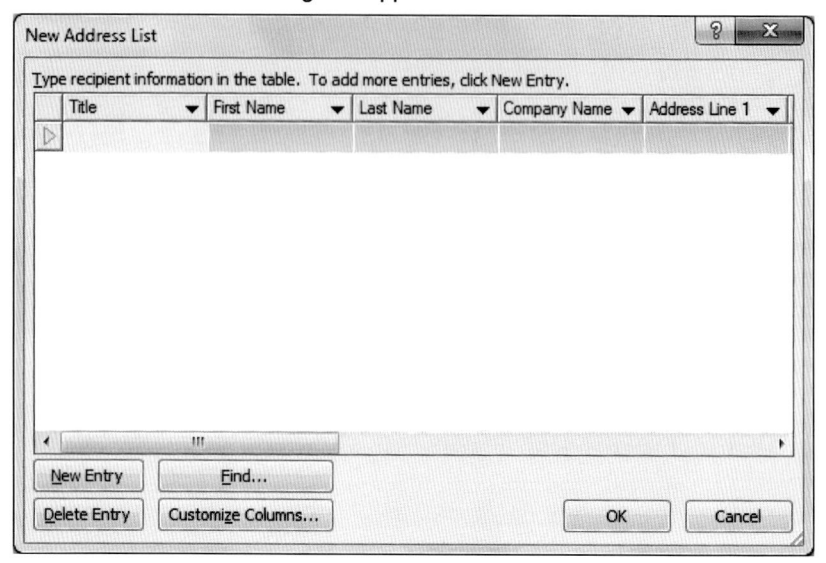

Figure 119

9. Select Customize Columns...

Figure 120

10. Edit Field Names as required

11. Select State, press Rename...

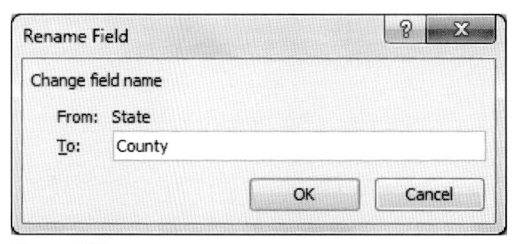

Figure 121

12. Type County, click [OK], edit the Customise Address List as below

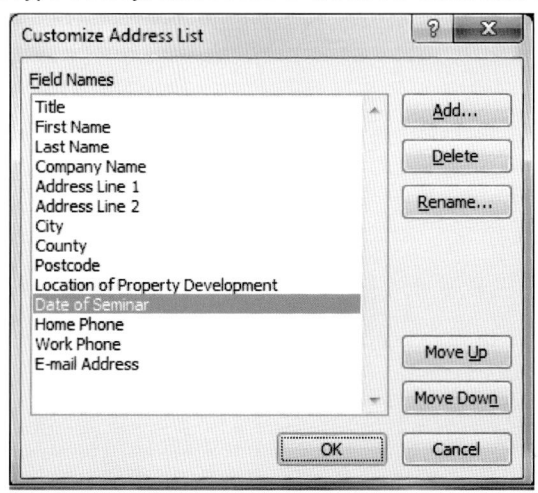

Figure 122

13. Add the following Field Names: Location of Property Development and Date of Seminar

14. Click [OK] to return to the New Address List

15. Enter the Address List as shown below

First Name	Last Name	Company Name	Address Line 1	Address Line 2	City	Post Code	Home Phone	Work Phone	Location of Property Development
Roy	Brown		7 Main Street		Sheffield	S60 2FF	0114 219 1234	0114 219 3456	Puerto Pollensa Mallorca
Marian	Longdale	Cottons Spa Limited	1 Chaffinch Road		Leeds	L1 2DF	0845 8900 7812	090 8900 7813	Alcudia Mallorca Spain
John	Bell	Knutsford Bridge Hotel	Macclesfield Lane		Lincoln	L6 9BV	0845 657731	01556 78921	Mondello Sicily Italy
Roger	Clarke	Northern Bell Company	Azric Drive		Bristol	BS32 1JK	01454 12234	01454 22564	Marbella Spain
Lucy	McDonald	Ullswater Lodge	11 Ullswater Lane	Penrith	Cumbria	CA11 9OJ	01768 1234	01768 2345	Seville Spain

Figure 123

16. In the Field Name: Location of Property Development, enter a different location for each person in the Address List
17. In the Field Name: Date of Seminar, enter a date
18. Click [OK], the Save Address List dialog appears
19. Save as Property Development Address List

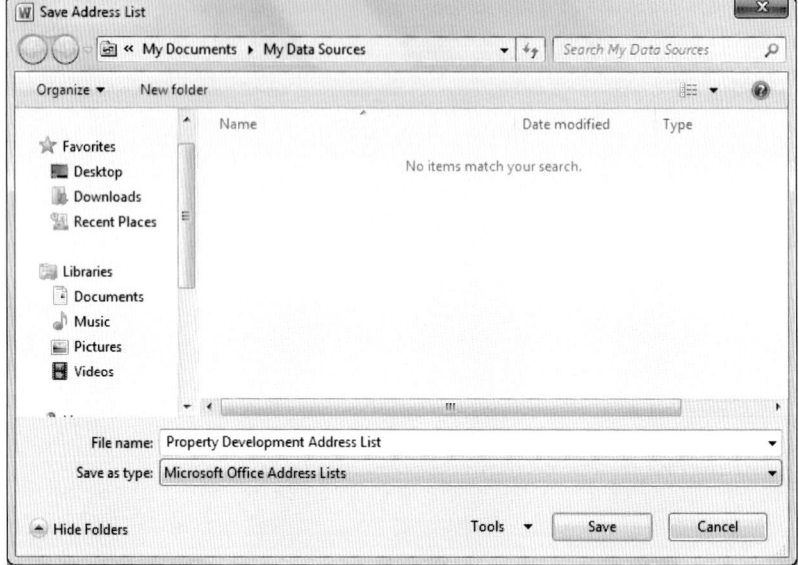

Figure 124

20. Click [Save], the Mail Merge Recipients dialog check list appears

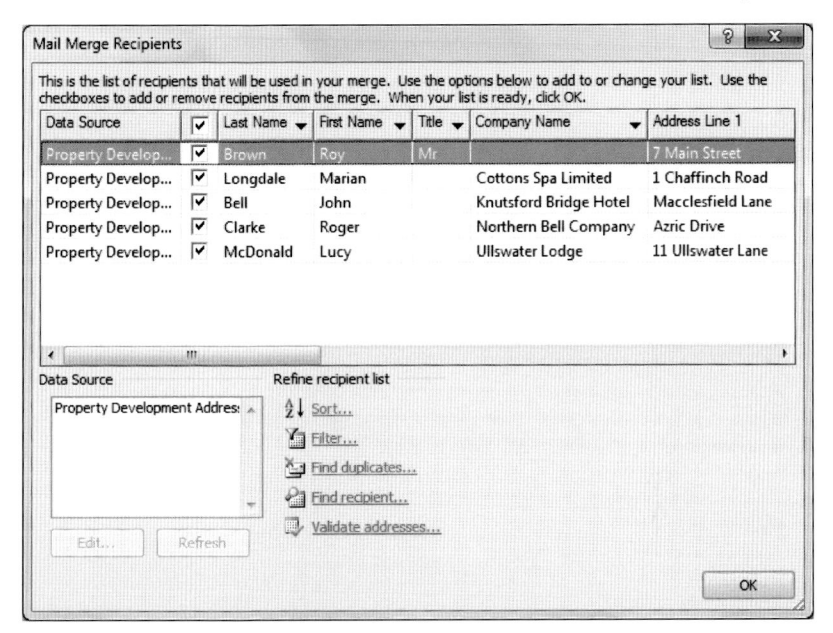

Figure 125

21. Check and edit the list as required
22. Select [OK], click on Next: Write your letter to move to Step 4

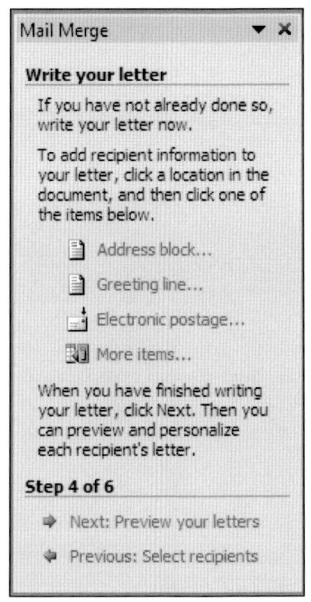

Figure 126

23. Type out the letter exactly as shown below

SMART Property Development
PO Box 80
Pedro Mas Y Reus
Puerto Pollensa
Mallorca
Telephone: 0800 123 456

03 April

As a valued customer of ours you are invited to join us on at the for a Property Development Seminar. The speaker will be Mr Charles Wright, covering the benefits of living abroad, followed by Miss Jennifer Lang, speaking about property management and development.

We would be pleased if you would telephone the office to confirm your attendance. We look forward to seeing you.

Yours sincerely

Charles Wright
SMART Property Development

Figure 127

24. Position the cursor where the address is to appear
25. Click on Address Block, the Insert Address Block dialog box appears

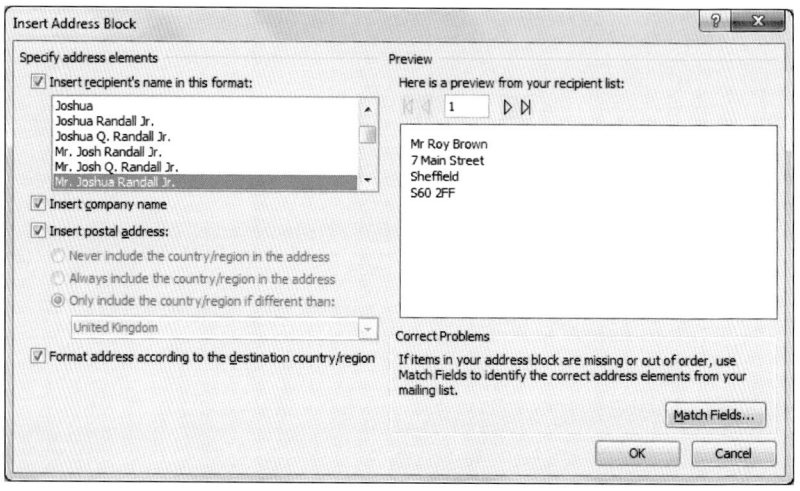

Figure 128

26. Select the required options, click `OK`
27. Position the cursor where the greeting line is to be placed

28. Select `Greeting line...`, the Insert Greeting Line dialog box appears

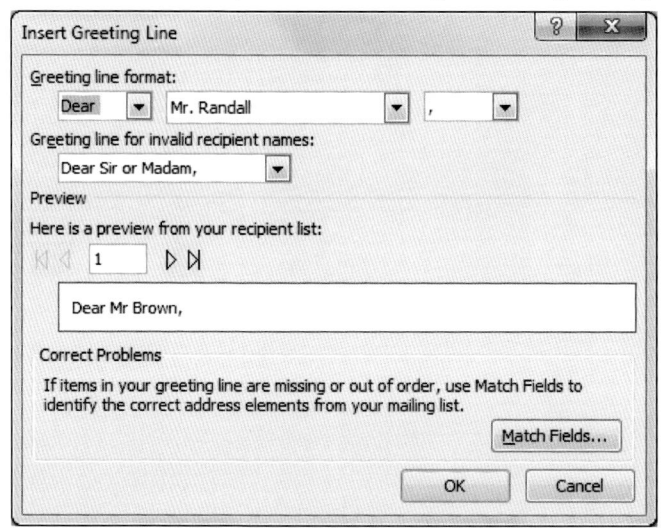

Figure 129

29. Select the required options, click `OK`
30. Place the cursor on the first line of the letter between the words **on** and **at**
31. Select `More items...`, choose Date of Seminar
32. Click `Insert`, press `Close`
33. Position the cursor between the words **the** and **for**
34. Select `More items...`, select Location of Property Development
35. Click `Insert`, press `Close`

36. Choose Next: Preview your letters to move to Step 5

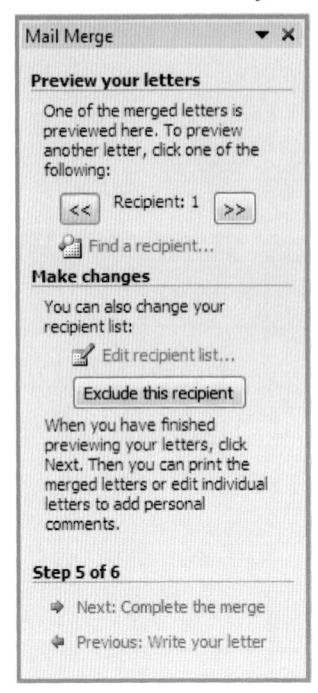

Figure 130

37. Step 5 enables you to preview and edit the final documents
38. Select Next: Complete the merge to move to Step 6

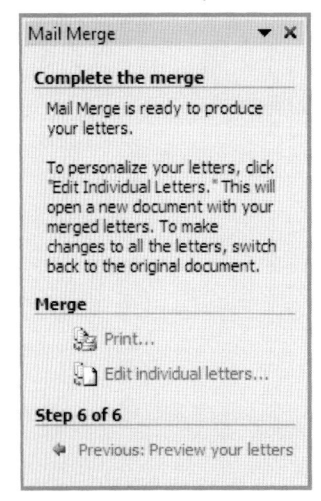

Figure 131

39. Select Edit individual letters
40. The Merge to New Document dialog box appears

Figure 132

41. Select **A**ll
42. Click `OK` the merged document appears on screen
43. Press `File`, `Print` to view the individual letters
44. Alternatively press `CTRL` `F2` to preview the pages
45. Select `Print`
46. Press `ESC` to go to Print Layout View

Creating Labels using Mail Merge

1. Open a new blank document
2. Select `Mailings`, `Start Mail Merge`, `Step by Step Mail Merge Wizard...`
3. choose Labels

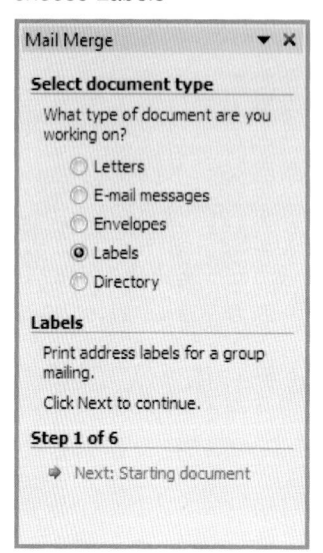

Figure 133

4. Select Next: Starting document to move to Step 2

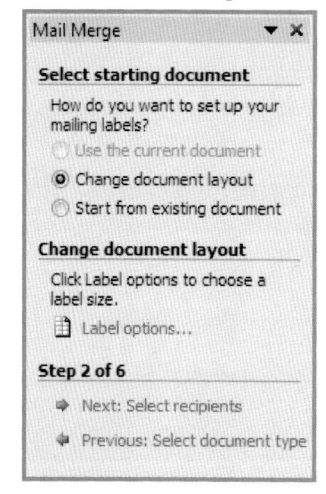

Figure 134

5. Select Change document layout, click [Label options...]
6. The Labels Options dialog box appears
7. Select the style of your labels, complete the options as shown below

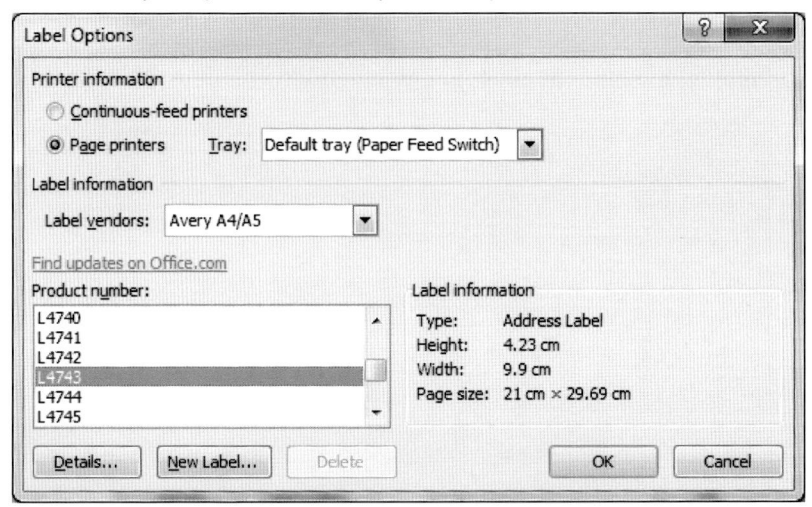

Figure 135

8. Click [Details...] to display more information on the label

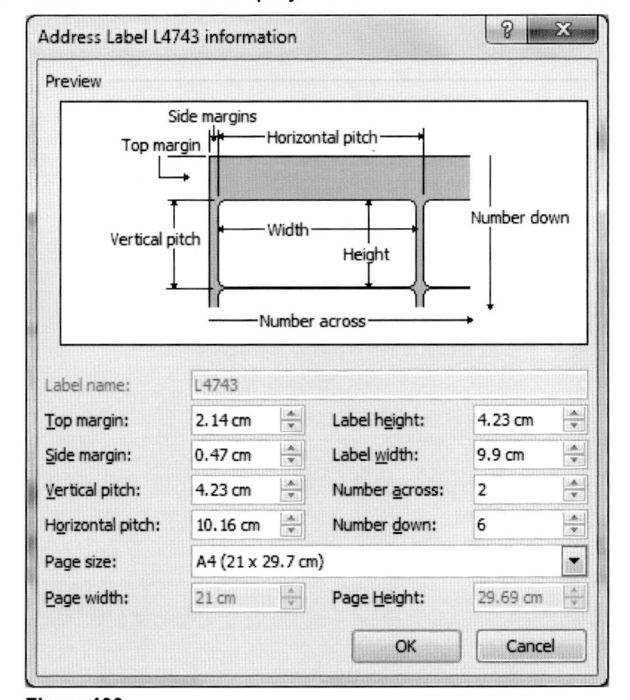

Figure 136

9. Press **OK** twice to return to the Mail Merge

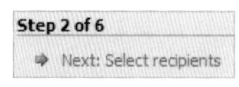

Figure 137

10. Press Next: Select recipients to move to Step 3

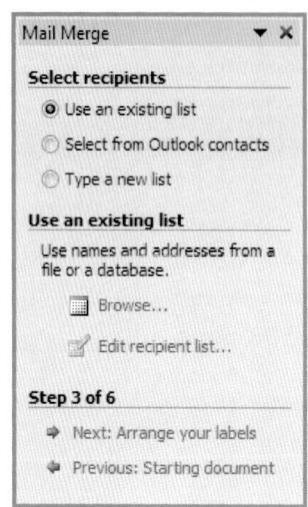

Figure 138

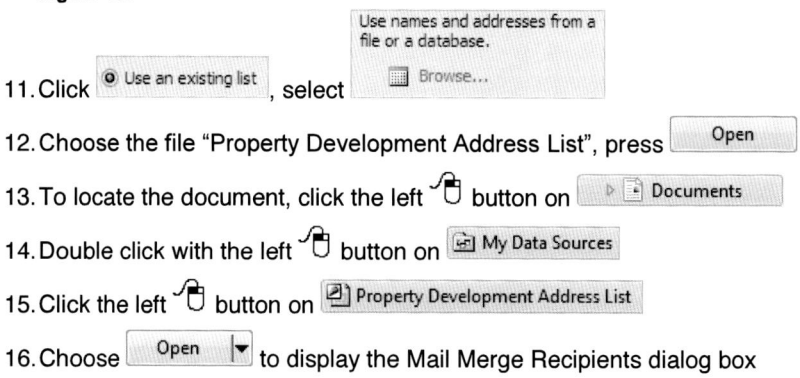

11. Click **Use an existing list**, select **Browse...**

12. Choose the file "Property Development Address List", press **Open**

13. To locate the document, click the left button on **Documents**

14. Double click with the left button on **My Data Sources**

15. Click the left button on **Property Development Address List**

16. Choose **Open** to display the Mail Merge Recipients dialog box

[Figure 139 - Mail Merge Recipients dialog box]

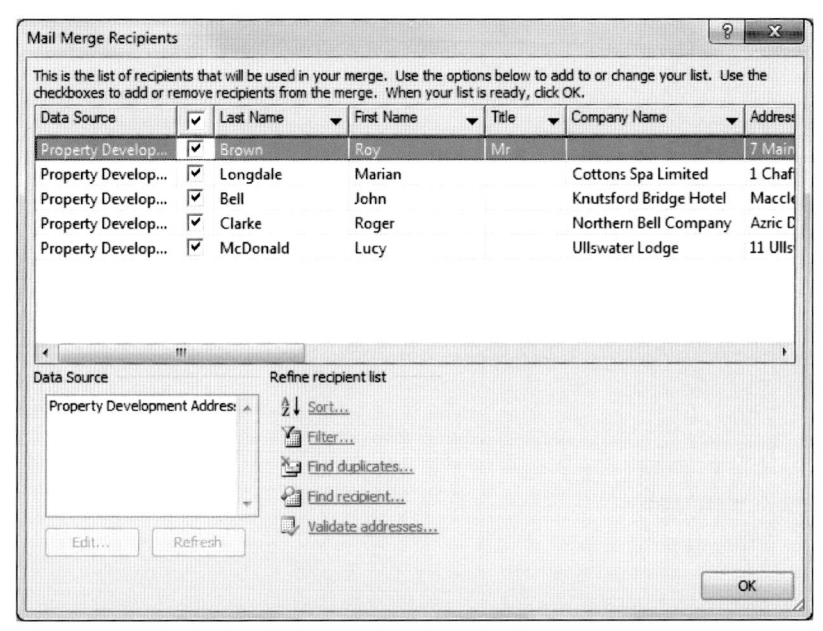

Figure 139

17. Deselect records not required by removing the ✓ with the left 🖱 button

18. Press [OK], click ➡ Next: Arrange your labels

[Figure 140 - Mail Merge task pane showing Step 3 of 6]

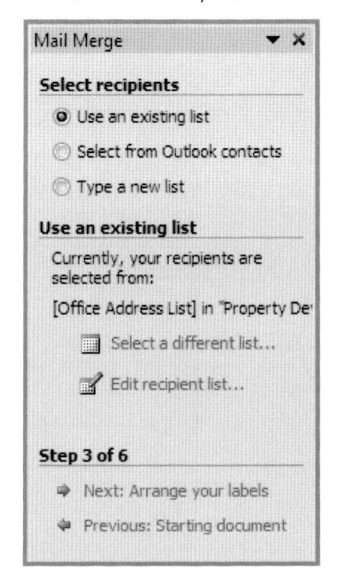

Figure 140

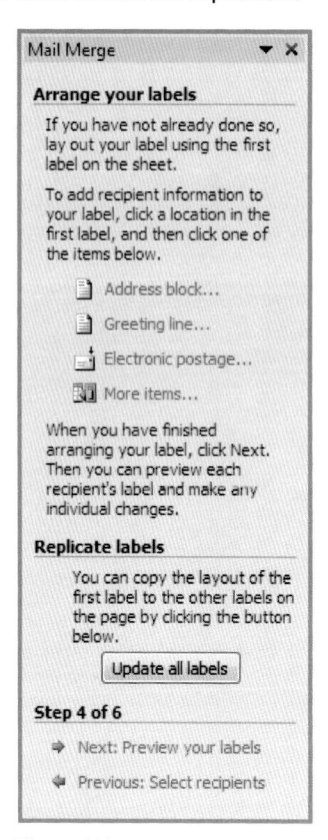

Figure 141

19. Select [Address block...]

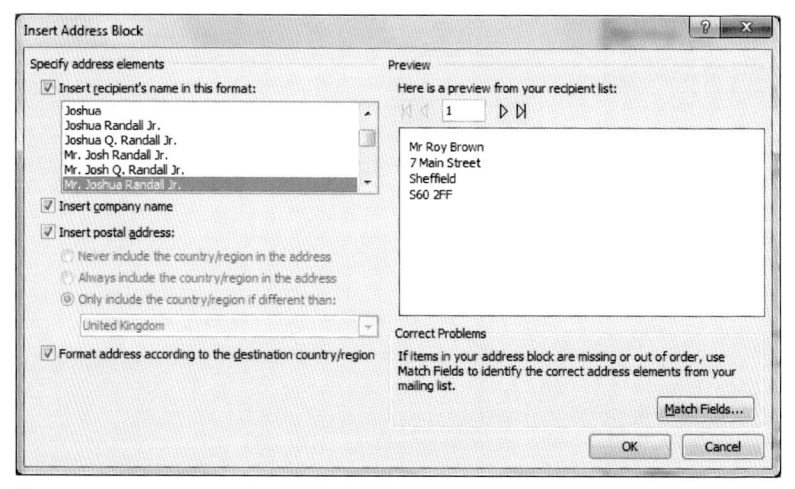

Figure 142

20. The Preview area displays the layout of your label
21. Choose **OK**
22. The flashing cursor appears after the **Address Block** in the first label
23. Select **Update all labels**

Replicate labels

You can copy the layout of the first label to the other labels on the page by clicking the button below.

Update all labels

Figure 143

24. Select **Next: Preview your labels**

Mail Merge

Preview your labels

Some of the merged labels are previewed here. To preview another label, click one of the following:

<< Recipient: 1 >>

Find a recipient...

Make changes

You can also change your recipient list:

Edit recipient list...

When you have finished previewing your labels, click Next. Then you can print the merged labels or edit individual labels to add personal comments.

Step 5 of 6

➡ Next: Complete the merge

⬅ Previous: Arrange your labels

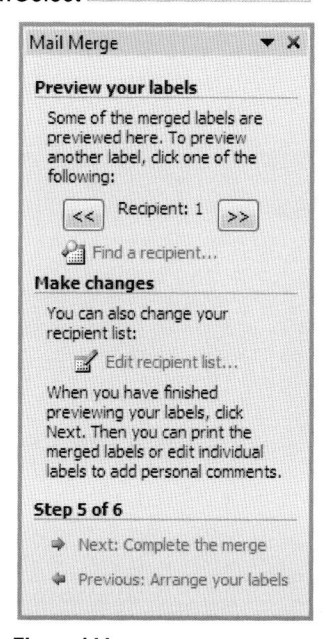

Figure 144

25. Choose `Next: Complete the merge`

Figure 145

26. Choose `Edit individual labels...` to merge the labels

Figure 146

27. Select the appropriate option
28. Click `OK`
29. Press `File`, `Print` to view the labels
30. Alternatively press `CTRL` `F2` to preview the pages
31. Select `Print`
32. Press `ESC` to go to Print Layout View

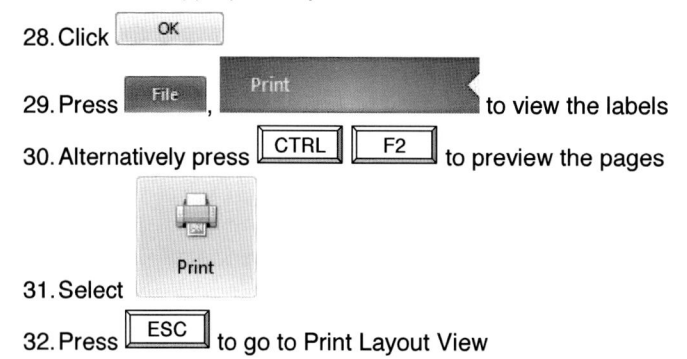

Exercise 12: - Creating Labels

1. Select Mailings, Labels
2. Create an address label for your organisation
3. Reproduce the labels so they appear all on one page in a new document
4. Preview the results
5. Save the document as Company Labels

Templates

A template is a means of creating a document that is consistent allowing such documents as letters, faxes and memos to be used with pre-set styles and formatting. When a new document is created based on a template it is used as the foundation for the new document.

Templates are saved to the Normal general area; however, it is possible to create a new tab for an organisation in the templates area that allows company templates to be quickly identified.

Save a Document as a Template

1. Open the document to be saved as a template
2. Select **File**, **Save As**
3. Name the template in the File **n**ame area
4. Ensure **Save as type: Word Template** is selected
5. Click the arrow at the top of the Save As Type dialog box to display the templates area
6. Click on

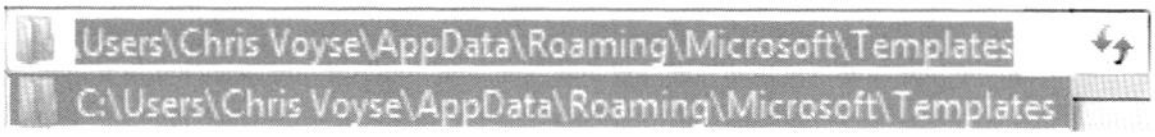

Figure 147

7. Select **New folder**
8. In File Name, type Smart PC Guides Templates, press **Enter**
9. Re select the Smart PC Guides folder, click **Open**

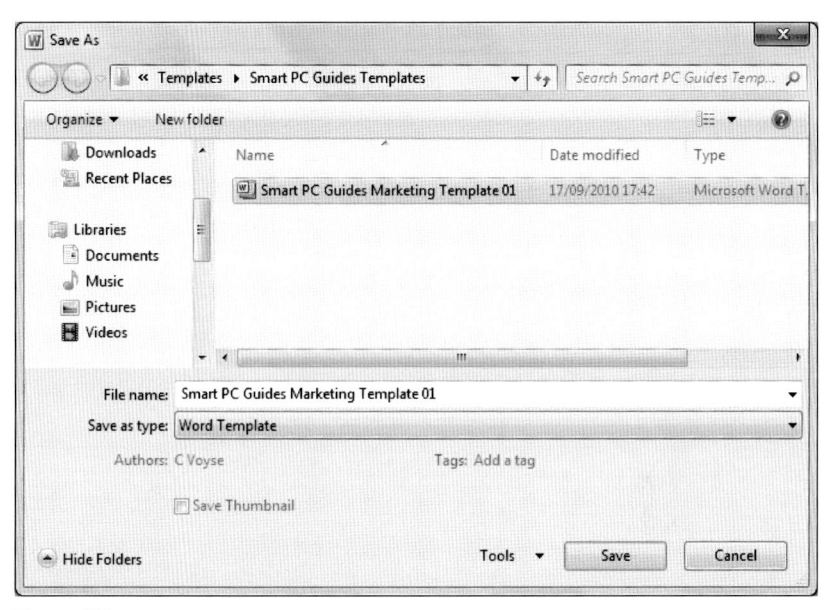

Figure 148

10. Save the template as Smart PC Guides Marketing Template 01
11. Click Save

View a Template

1. Select **File**, **New**, **My templates**
2. Choose the **Smart PC Guides Templates** Tab

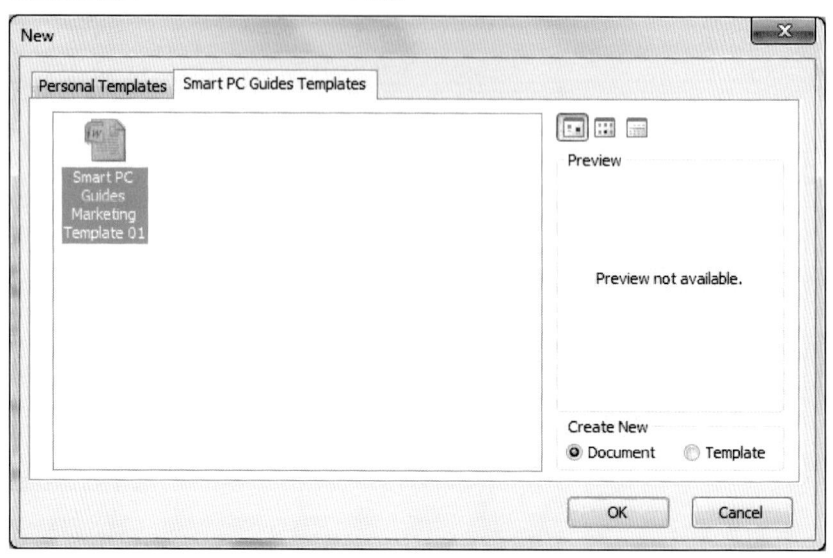

Figure 149

3. Select the Smart PC Guides Marketing Template 01
4. A new document based on the template is created
5. Click **OK**

Open and Amend an existing Template

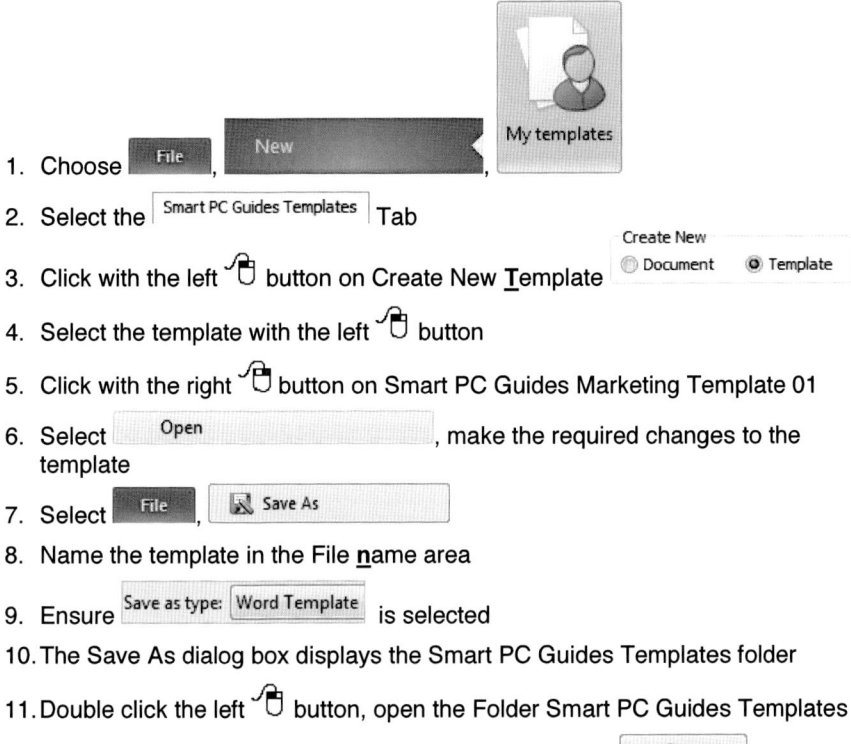

1. Choose **File**, **New**, **My templates**
2. Select the **Smart PC Guides Templates** Tab
3. Click with the left button on Create New **T**emplate (Create New: ◯ Document ◉ Template)
4. Select the template with the left button
5. Click with the right button on Smart PC Guides Marketing Template 01
6. Select **Open**, make the required changes to the template
7. Select **File**, **Save As**
8. Name the template in the File **n**ame area
9. Ensure **Save as type: Word Template** is selected
10. The Save As dialog box displays the Smart PC Guides Templates folder
11. Double click the left button, open the Folder Smart PC Guides Templates
12. Select Smart PC Guides Marketing Template 01, click **Save**
13. The following dialog box appears

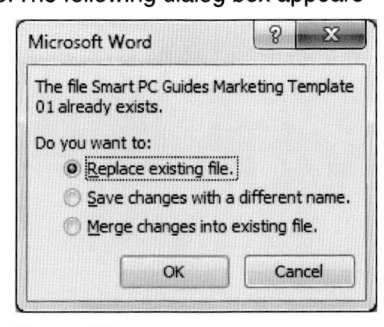

Figure 150

14. In this case select replace the existing file, press **OK**, close the document
15. From My Templates area open a new document based on the Smart PC Guides Marketing Template 01, the changes have been applied

Accessibility Checker

The Accessibility Checker is new to 2010 and allows the user to identify potential difficulties that people with disabilities may have when reading a document. The Accessibility Checker generates a list of errors and possible fixes and also helps screen readers understand the content in a document.

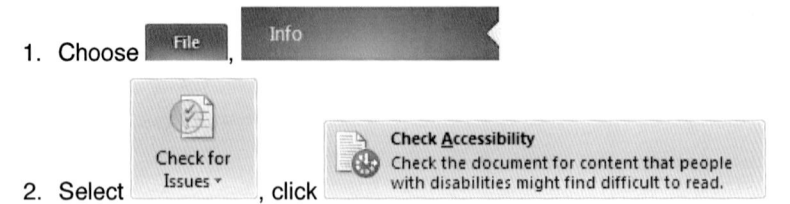

1. Choose **File**, **Info**
2. Select **Check for Issues**, click **Check Accessibility** – Check the document for content that people with disabilities might find difficult to read.
3. The Accessibility Checker summary outlining possible errors appears on the right hand side of the screen in the task pane area

Figure 151

4. If an error is showing under `Inspection Results`
5. Select the error to find where it is located

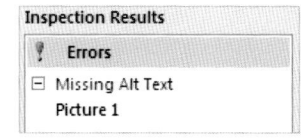

Figure 152

6. Additional Information explains why the error should be fixed and how to fix it

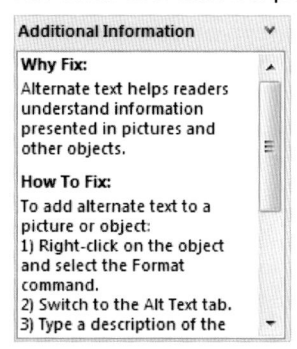

Figure 153

7. To add alternative text, right click on the object or item in the document, for example Picture 1
8. Select `Format Picture...`
9. The Format Shape dialog box appears

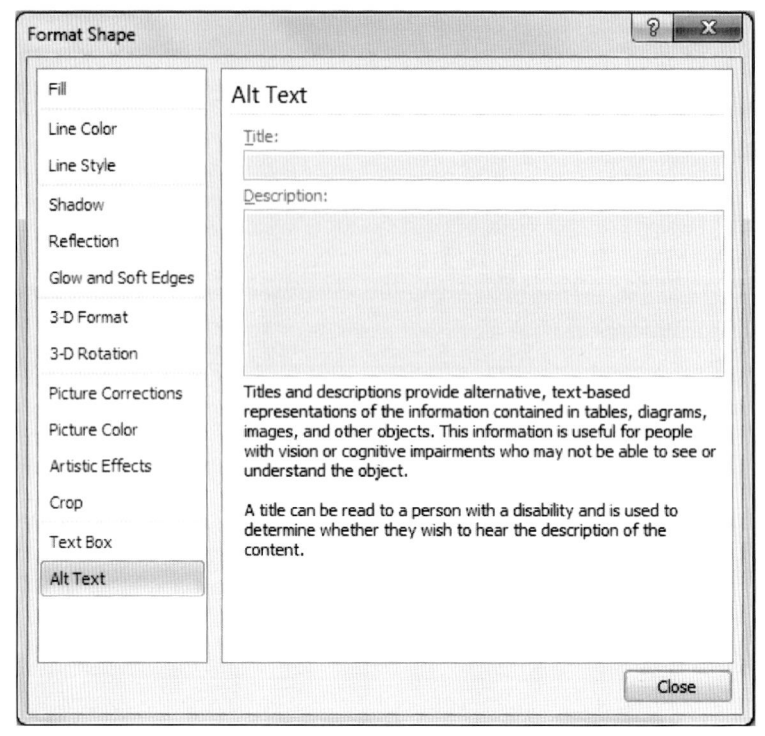

Figure 154

10. Select Alt Text

11. Enter a title and description, click Close

12. Close the Accessibility Checker panel when all the errors have been completed

13. Save the document

Section 3
Expert Level Objectives

	Pages
• Outline View	130
• Master Documents	135
• Form Design	138
• Introduction to Macros	156
• Watermarks	163
• Hyperlinks	167
• Columns	170
• Linking Information with other MS Products	174
• Inserting Pictures and Graphics	176
• Drawing Tools	183
• Working with Text Boxes	185
• Footnotes and Endnotes	189
• Shortcut Keys	192

Outline View

Outline View allows a document's structure to be seen when the document has been created using Styles and Formatting. The document can be collapsed or expanded to view headings and specific parts of the document to allow quick and easy re-organisation by moving, copying or dragging headings and text. If the document contains a Table of Contents and changes have been made to the document, this can be updated in Outline View.

Outline Commands

1. Open a new document
2. Select View, Outline from the Document Views Grouping
3. The Outlining Commands appear

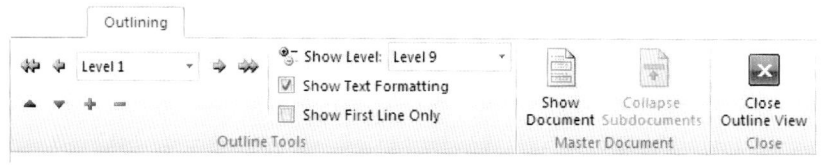

Figure 155

Outlining an Existing Document

1. Open a new document, create the following text using Styles and Formatting
2. Construct the document using Heading Styles 1-3 and a numbering list
3. Save the document as Working in Outline View

Note: The document that has been created below contained additional text that has been collapsed identified by the ⊕ sign. The document you have created will contain a ⊖ sign.

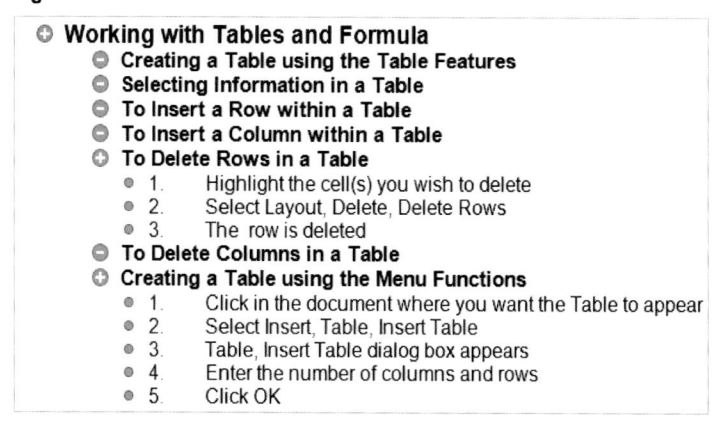

- ⊕ **Working with Tables and Formula**
    - ⊖ Creating a Table using the Table Features
    - ⊖ Selecting Information in a Table
    - ⊖ To Insert a Row within a Table
    - ⊖ To Insert a Column within a Table
    - ⊕ To Delete Rows in a Table
        - 1. Highlight the cell(s) you wish to delete
        - 2. Select Layout, Delete, Delete Rows
        - 3. The row is deleted
    - ⊖ To Delete Columns in a Table
    - ⊕ Creating a Table using the Menu Functions
        - 1. Click in the document where you want the Table to appear
        - 2. Select Insert, Table, Insert Table
        - 3. Table, Insert Table dialog box appears
        - 4. Enter the number of columns and rows
        - 5. Click OK

Figure 156

4. Select Outline View
5. Click with the left [mouse] button on the word Formula in the title heading
6. Press the [↓] key to the end of the document
7. As you scroll the Heading Style Level changes to the defined styles

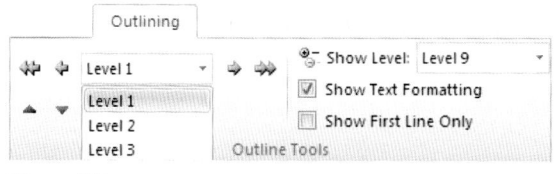

Figure 157

8. Select [Show Level: Level 2] from the Outlining Tools Command
9. The document is collapsed showing Heading Styles 1 and 2
10. Click with the left [mouse] button on the [+] in the Ribbon to display the hidden item
11. Press the [−] to collapse the selected item
12. Alternatively double click with the left [mouse] button on the plus sign ⊕ in the document to collapse or expand the section
13. Select [Show Level: All Levels] to display all the items

Promote and Demote Information

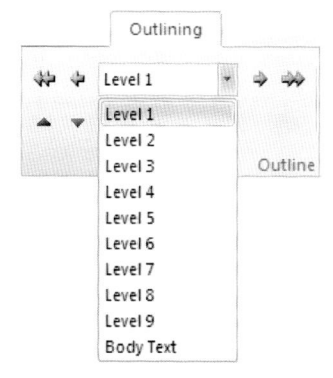

Figure 158

1. Place the cursor in a heading style, click the Promote to Heading 1 icon
2. The style is automatically changed to Heading 1
3. Select the Demote to Body Text icon to change the style to Body Text or the Normal default style
4. The Promote icon moves forward to the next highest level
5. The Demote icon moves backwards to the next lowest level
6. Alternatively select the Outline icon

Move Information in Outline View

1. Select Move Up to move information upwards to a new location
2. Choose Move Down to move information downwards
3. Select Expand to expand selected items
4. Choose Collapse to collapse the selected item

Note: All collapsed information is kept with the heading when being moved to a new location in Outline View.

Exercise 13: - Working with a Table of Contents

```
                    Table of Contents
Monday ............................................................................... 2
    Briefing at 10:00 .......................................................... 2
Tuesday .............................................................................. 3
    Performance Review at 15:00 ..................................... 3
Wednesday ......................................................................... 4
        Progress Meeting 09:30 ......................................... 4
Thursday ............................................................................. 5
    Staff Appraisal at 14:15 ................................................ 5
Friday ................................................................................... 6
        Company Car New Criteria ..................................... 6
```

1. Generate the Table of Contents shown above
2. Select **References**, **Update Table**
3. Scroll to the beginning of the table
4. Change Briefing at 10:00 to Normal Style
5. Change Company Car New Criteria to Heading Style 3
6. Click **Update Table**
7. Select Update **e**ntire table

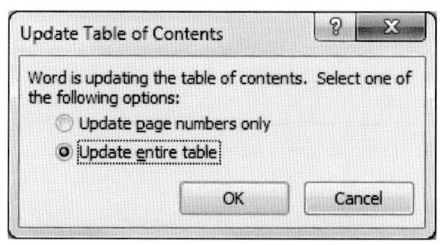

8. Click **OK** to view the updated Table of Contents
9. Close and save the document as Generating a Table of Contents

Outlined Numbered List

The Outline Number feature automatically indents lists of items at different levels.

1. Open a new document
2. Select `Home`, choose Multilevel List from the Paragraph Grouping

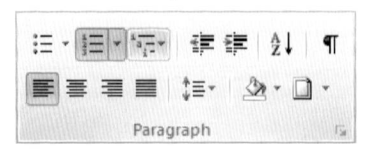

Figure 159

3. Choose the option highlighted below from the List Library gallery

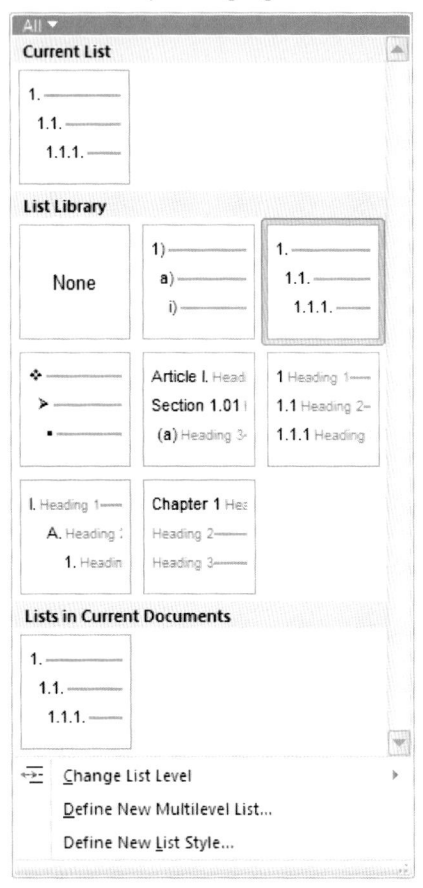

Figure 160

> 1. Microsoft does the work for you
>   1.1. No Business can work without the technology of today
>   1.1.1. This is never truer, than when it comes to needing a reliable word processing system..........................
>   1.1.2. The busy office requires all of the tools of today's technology to help it work effectively............
> 2. Accounting at the touch of a button
>   2.1.|

Figure 161

4. Type out the text above
5. Press [Enter] and [TAB] to move in a level
6. To move back a level press [SHIFT] and [TAB]

Master Documents

A Master Document is used to organise and maintain long documents by dividing it into Subdocuments that are managed by links to the Master Document.

Creating a Master Document

1. Create a folder named Master Documents
2. Open a new document
3. Select Outline View, the Outlining commands appears

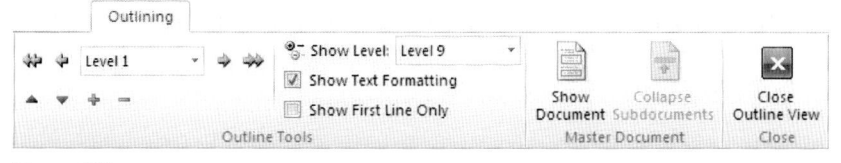

Figure 162

4. Select Level 1 from the Outlining commands, this represents Heading Style 1
5. Type Demonstration of Master Documents, press [Enter]
6. Select Body Text, this represents Normal style
7. Type the text below

> "The following example demonstrates the creation of Master Documents, inserting subdocuments, moving subdocuments in the Master Document, adding a new subdocument to the Master Document and deleting a subdocument"

Figure 163

8. Press `Enter`
9. Switch to Print Layout View, click on the Styles Window icon
10. Return to the Outline View, the Styles window is displayed

11. Select Level 1, type Chapter 1, press `Enter`
12. Select Level 2, type Inserting a Subdocument, press `Enter`
13. Create Chapters 2 and 3
14. Highlight Chapter 1 and the Normal body text associated with it
15. Click with the left button on `Show Document`
16. The Master Document Grouping is expanded

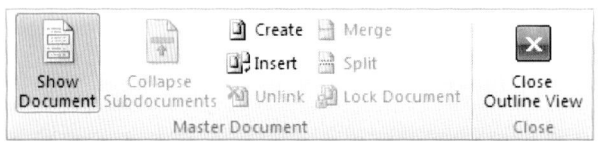

Figure 164

17. Click on the Create Subdocument icon `Create`
18. Repeat the steps to create subdocuments for the other Chapters
19. Save the document as Demonstration of Master Documents in the Master Documents Folder
20. Close the document

Opening a Subdocument

1. Open the folder Master Documents Folder
2. Open the subdocument Chapter 1
3. Add some additional text, save and close the document

Inserting a Subdocument

1. Open a new document, select View , Outline
2. Select Level 1, type Chapter 4, press Enter
3. Select Level 2 Heading Style 2, type Adding a New Document, press Enter
4. Select the Body Text Level Normal Style, type the following text

   "This demonstrates creating a new document and adding it to the Master Documents".

   Figure 165

5. Save the document as Chapter 4 in the Master Documents folder
6. Close the document
7. Re-open the document named Demonstration of Master Documents

   Demonstration of Master Documents
   - The following example demonstrates the creation of Master Documents, inserting subdocuments, moving subdocuments in the Master Document, adding a new subdocument to the Master Document and deleting a subdocument.
   - C:\Users\ChrisVoyse\Documents\Master Documents\Chapter 1.docx
   - C:\Users\ChrisVoyse\Documents\Master Documents\Chapter 2.docx
   - C:\Users\ChrisVoyse\Documents\Master Documents\Chapter 3.docx

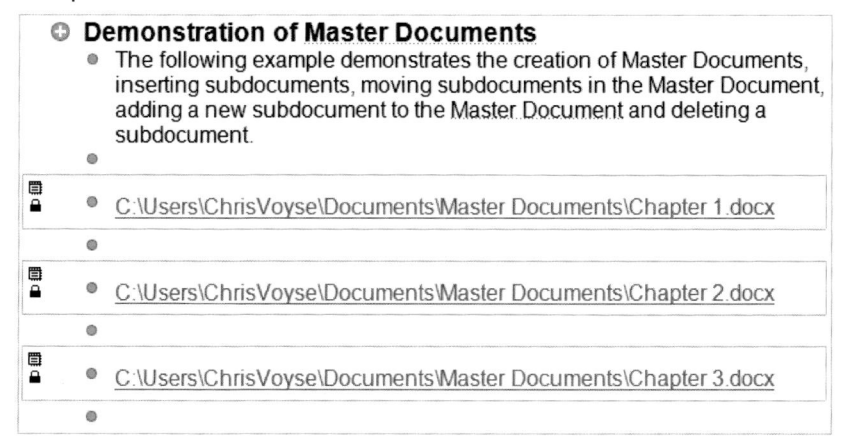

   Figure 166

8. The Subdocuments appear in a collapsed form
9. Click on Expand Subdocuments
10. Ensure the cursor is positioned at the end of the document
11. Click with the left button on Insert Subdocument icon Insert
12. The Insert Subdocument dialog box appears

13. Select the document Chapter 4, click **Open**
14. Chapter 4 is incorporated into the Master Document
15. Save and close the Master Document

Moving a Subdocument

1. Open the document Demonstration of Master Documents, select the subdocument to be moved
2. Click and hold down the left button on the subdocument icon positioned in the top left hand corner of the subdocument box

   • C:\Users\ChrisVoyse\Documents\Master Documents\Chapter 1.docx

   Figure 167

3. Drag the subdocument to a new location

Note: Double click on the subdocument icon to open an individual document, to return to the Demonstration of Master Documents, close that particular individual document.

Delete a Subdocument

1. Expand the Master Document, select the subdocument to be deleted
2. Click on the Subdocument icon to highlight the document
3. Press **Delete**

Lock and Unlock Subdocuments

If another person tries to work on a subdocument that is already in use, the subdocument is automatically locked to others. Password protection could be applied to the subdocument. See the section on Password Protection.

Form Commands

Text can be inserted into documents using Form Fields that are created by Drop-Down Form Fields or Check Box Form Fields. This is useful when a form is to be filled out on screen allowing Status Bar Text and Help Text Fields to assist users to complete the form electronically. Forms can be designed with a variety of formats using text and numbers and by setting the maximum length of each field or size.

Exercise 14: - Creating a Form using the Form Commands

Training Needs Analysis Form

Name:

Employers Name:

Daytime Telephone Number:

Mobile Number:

Contact Address:

Address Line 2:

Town/City:

Postcode:

Country:

Select a Course of Interest:

Microsoft Word	Microsoft Excel	Microsoft PowerPoint
Foundation	Foundation	Foundation
Intermediate	Intermediate	Intermediate
Expert	Expert	Expert

Tick the following areas of interest

Voice Recognition

Facial Recognition

Handwriting Recognition

1. Open a new document
2. Using a table create the Training Needs Analysis Form shown above
3. Save the form as a template named Training Needs Analysis Form

Inserting Text Form Fields

1. Click **File**, **Options**, **Customize Ribbon**
2. In the Choose Commands from area select the downward arrow
3. Select **All Commands**
4. Click with the left button on Developer, click the plus sign
5. This expands the selection, click the plus sign on Controls

```
☐ Controls
    Aa  Rich Text Content Control
    Aa  Plain Text Content Control
        Picture Content Control
        Building Block Gallery Content C
        Combo Box Content Control
        Drop-Down List Content Control
        Date Picker Content Control
        Check Box Content Control
        Legacy Tools
        Design Mode
        Properties
    ⊞   Group
```

Figure 168

6. Click with the left button on the minus sign to collapse the controls
7. Click a second time on the minus sign to collapse the Developer options
8. Click the left button on **Add >>** to Add the Developer Tools to the Main Tab
9. Click **OK** to close the Word Options dialog box
10. The Developer Tab is displayed on the Ribbon

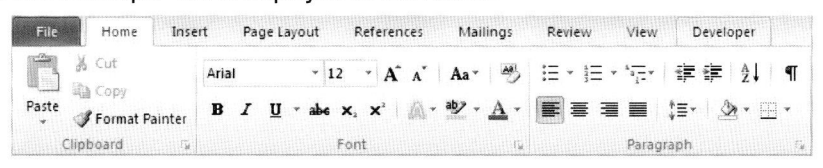

Figure 169

11. Select the Developer Tab **Developer**
12. Choose Legacy Tools from the Controls Grouping
13. Select the Form Field Shading icon

14. To deselect the shading, click on the Form Field Shading icon
15. Click with the left button where the Text Form Field is to appear
16. Choose Text Form Field from the Legacy Tools menu
17. Create the Form Fields for the rest of the form
18. Centre align the Text Form Fields
19. Save the form

Inserting Check Box Form Fields

1. Select the Developer Tab
2. Choose Legacy Tools from the Controls Grouping
3. Select the Form Field Shading icon
4. To deselect the shading, click on the Form Field Shading icon
5. Click with the left button where the Check Box Form Field is to appear
6. Choose from the Legacy Tools menu
7. Create the Check Box Form Fields for the rest of the form
8. Save the form

Training Needs Analysis Form

Name:	{FORMTEXT}
Employers Name:	{FORMTEXT}
Daytime Telephone Number:	{FORMTEXT}
Mobile Number:{FORMCHECKBOX}	{FORMTEXT}
Contact Address:	{FORMTEXT}
Address Line 2:	{FORMTEXT}
Town/City:	{FORMTEXT}
Postcode:	{FORMTEXT}
Country:	{FORMTEXT}
Select a Course of Interest:	{FORMDROPDOWN}

Microsoft Word	Microsoft Excel	Microsoft PowerPoint
Foundation	Foundation	Foundation
Intermediate	Intermediate	Intermediate
Expert	Expert	Expert

Tick the following areas of interest

Voice Recognition	{FORMCHECKBOX}
Facial Recognition	{FORMCHECKBOX}
Handwriting Recognition	{FORMCHECKBOX}

Figure 170

Customising Text Form Fields

The Text Form Fields can be customised using a variety of options such as regular text, number, date, current date, current time, calculations, length, field settings and help keys.

1. Click on the first Text Form Field to be customised
2. Select the `Developer` Tab, choose `Properties` from the Controls Grouping
3. The following dialog box appears

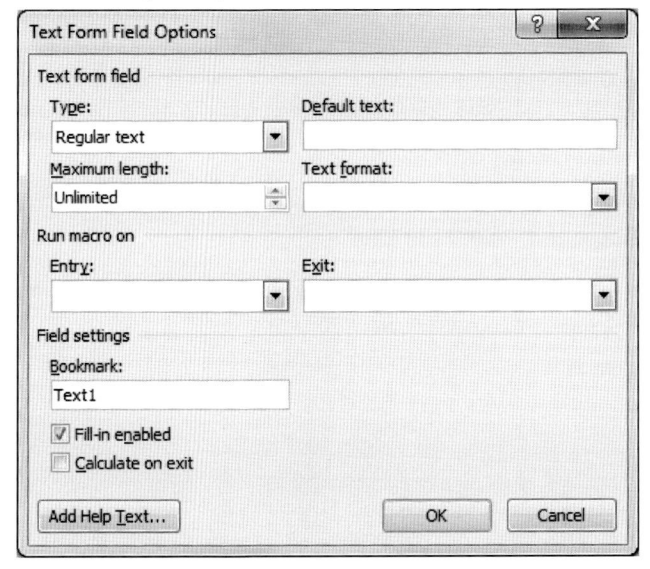

Figure 171

4. In the Type box, click on the ▼ arrow, select Regular text
5. Click on `Add Help Text...`

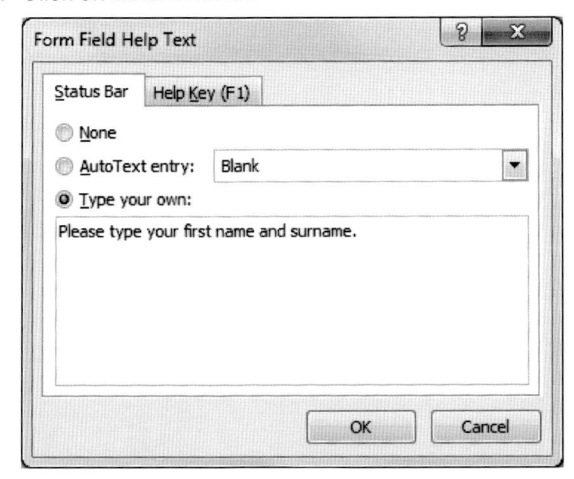

Figure 172

6. In the Type your own box type, Please type your first name and surname

7. Select [Help Key (F1)] Tab
8. In the Type your own box type, Please type your first name and surname
9. Click [OK] twice
10. Repeat the process to customise the other Text Form Fields
11. Save the form

Note: If using numbers in a Text Form Field, select the numbering option and select the maximum length required. The Number Format lets you choose several different formats to control how the numbers will be displayed.

Customising Check Box Form Fields

1. Highlight the Check Box Form Field Mobile Number
2. Select [Properties] from the Controls Grouping
3. The Check Box Form Field Options dialog box appears

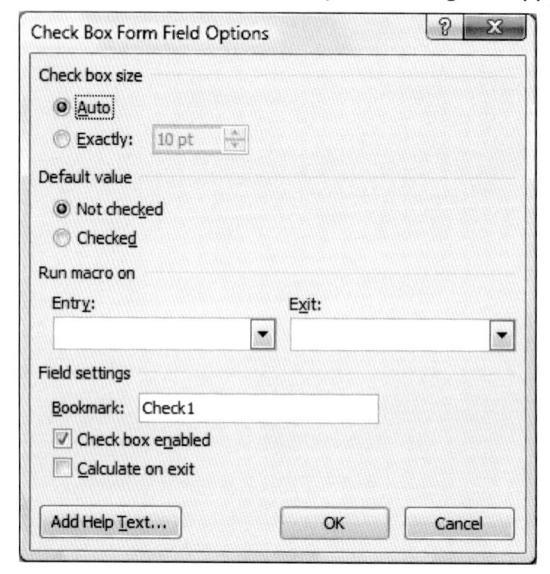

Figure 173

4. Click on [Add Help Text...]

5. Select the **S**tatus Bar Tab, type the text as shown below

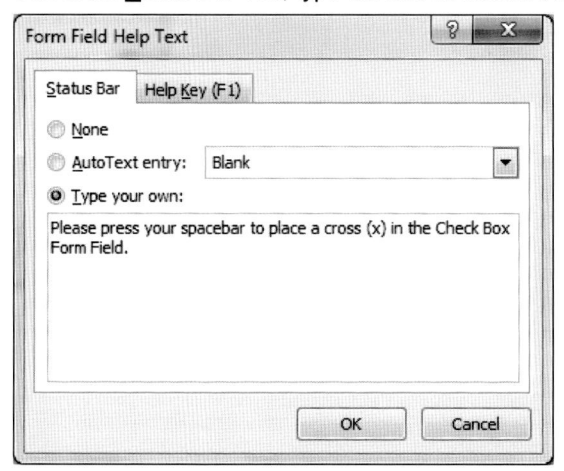

Figure 174

6. Select the Help **K**ey (F1) Tab type the text as shown below

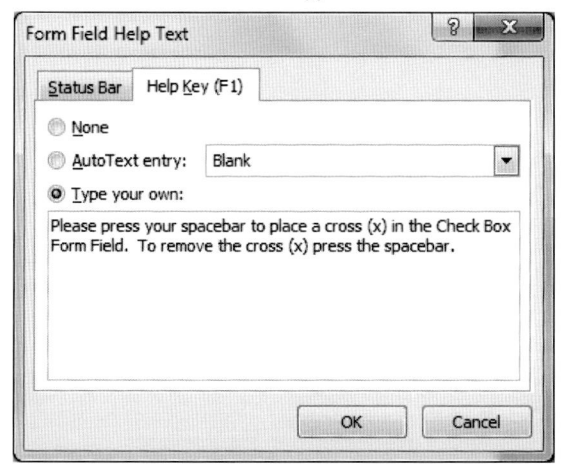

Figure 175

7. Click OK twice to return to the document

Protecting Forms

A document or template that contains Form Fields must be protected in order for the fields to be activated. When the form is ready to be protected

1. Select the `Developer` Tab, press `Restrict Editing`
2. The Restrict Formatting and Editing Task Pane appears

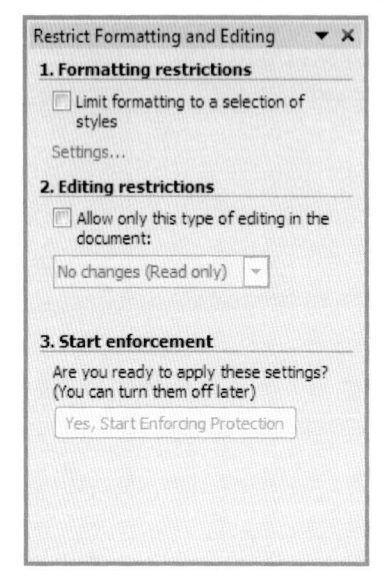

Figure 176

3. Click with the left button on `Design Mode` to switch off the Design Mode
4. Alternatively press `ALT` `L` `D` `M` to switch the Design Mode on or off
5. Place a tick ☑ in Allow only this type of editing in the document
6. Choose `Filling in forms` from the Editing restrictions menu
7. Select `Yes, Start Enforcing Protection`, the Start Enforcing Protection dialog box appears

Figure 177

8. Press `OK` to protect the document

Figure 178

9. To unprotect the document, click with the left 🖰 button on [Stop Protection]
10. If a password has been set the following dialog box appears

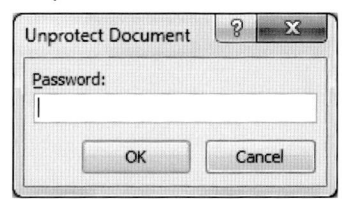

Figure 179

11. Press [OK], the document is unprotected

Note: A form can be protected without using passwords, however if a user clicks on unprotect, the form can be altered. When using passwords remember passwords should be more than 8 characters in length using letters, numbers and symbols. **WRITE DOWN THE PASSWORD USED AND KEEP IT IN A SECURE PLACE TO ENABLE ACCESS TO BE GAINED WHEN NECESSARY.**

AutoText Entries

1. Open a new document
2. Type out and right align your address, highlight the address
3. Select **Insert**, **Quick Parts ▾**, **Save Selection to Quick Part Gallery...**
4. The Create New Building Block dialog box appears
5. Complete the box as shown below

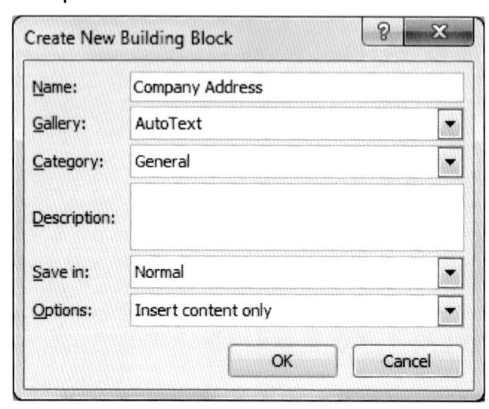

Figure 180

6. Click **OK**
7. Open a new document
8. Select, **Insert**, **Quick Parts ▾**, **Building Blocks Organizer...**
9. Choose the required address

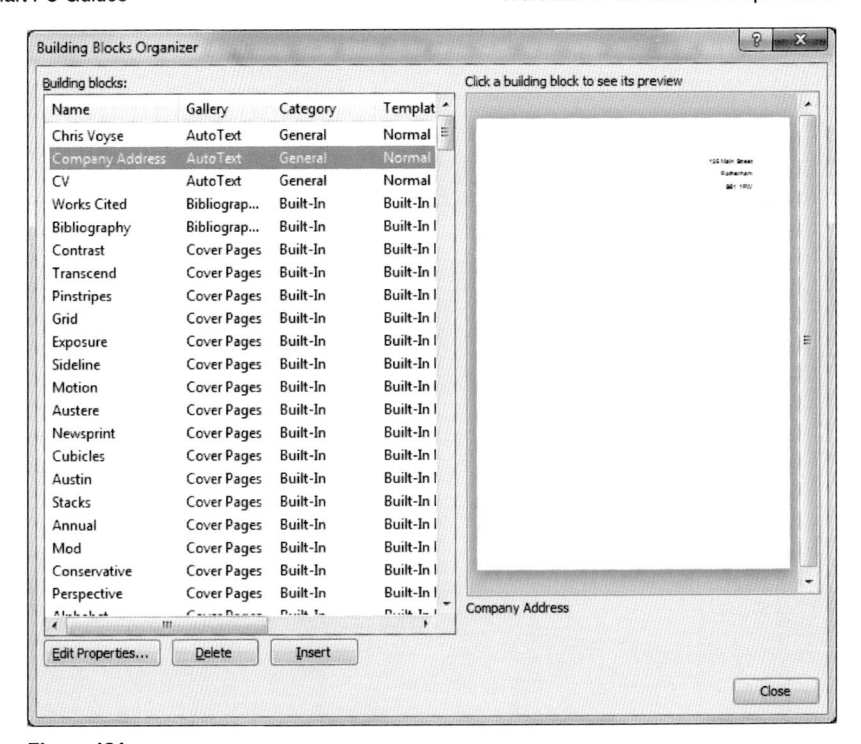

Figure 181

10. Click `Insert`, the address is inserted in the document

11. Alternatively press `ALT` `N` `Q` `B` to access the Building Block Organiser

Date Fields

1. Working in the same document, place the cursor where the date is to appear
2. Select `Insert`, `Quick Parts`, `Field...`
3. Alternatively press `ALT` `N` `Q` `F`
4. Select **C**ategories: choose All
5. In the **F**ield Names select Date and Time, choose Date

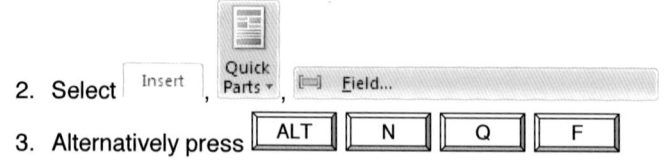

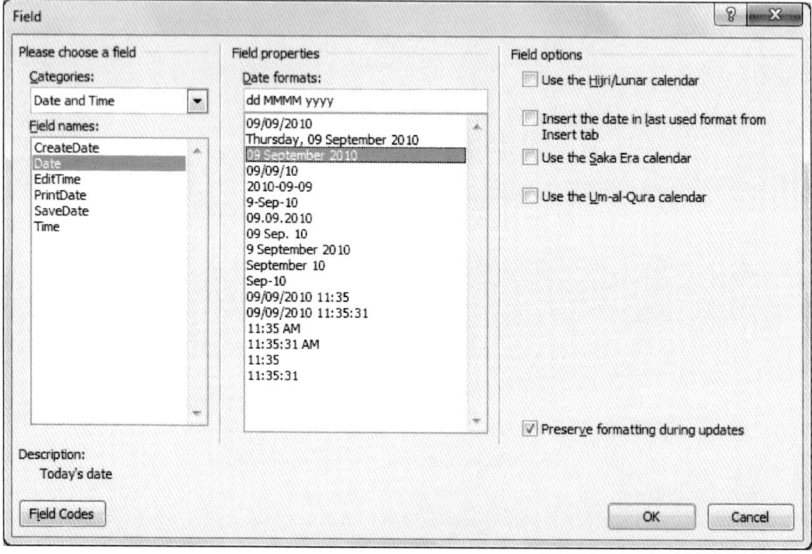

Figure 182

6. In **D**ate formats: select the required format, click `OK`
7. The date appears in the document, click on the date
8. Press `ALT` `F9` to view the field code

{ DATE \@ "dd MMMM yyyy" * MERGEFORMAT }

Figure 183

9. Press `ALT` `F9` to return to the document, save the document
10. Alternatively press `CTRL` `F9`
11. Type { DATE \@ "dd MMMM yyyy" * MERGEFORMAT } between the brackets
12. Press `CTRL` `A` to highlight the document, click `ALT` `F9` to display the date

AutoText List

1. Click in the document where you want a salutation to appear
2. Select Insert, Quick Parts, Field...
3. Select Categories, choose (All)
4. In Field names, choose AutoTextList, click in the New value: box
5. Type the salutation required

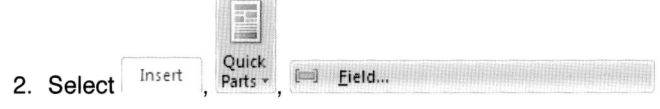

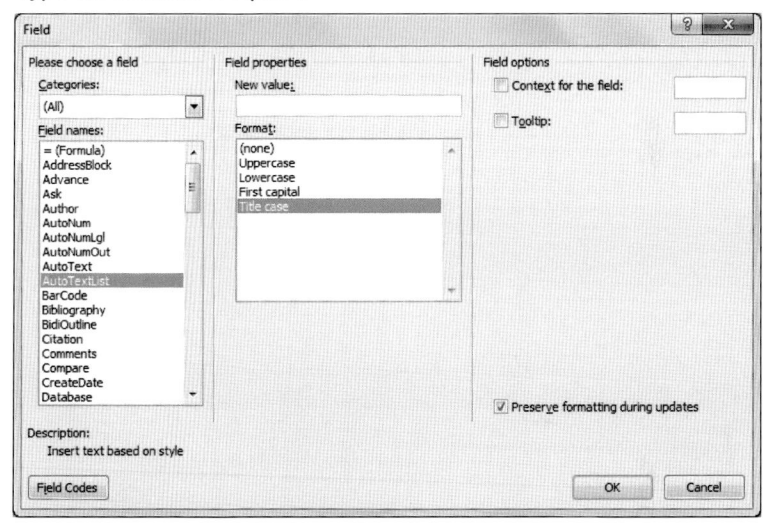

Figure 184

6. In the Format box, select Title case
7. Choose Field Codes to view the Advanced field properties

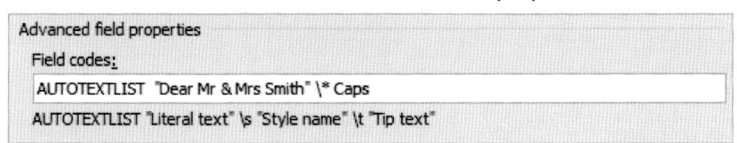

   Advanced field properties
   Field codes:
   AUTOTEXTLIST "Dear Mr & Mrs Smith" * Caps
   AUTOTEXTLIST "Literal text" \s "Style name" \t "Tip text"

Figure 185

8. Click OK, the following field appears in the document

   { AUTOTEXTLIST * Caps * MERGEFORMAT }

Figure 186

9. Press ALT F9, Dear Mr & Mrs Smith appears in the document
10. Save the changes to the document

Ask Field

The ASK Field is used at the beginning of a document to instruct the user to input data at other locations in the document in conjunction with Bookmarks.

1. Ensure the cursor is positioned where text is to be inserted
2. Select Insert, Quick Parts, Field...
3. In Field names: choose Ask

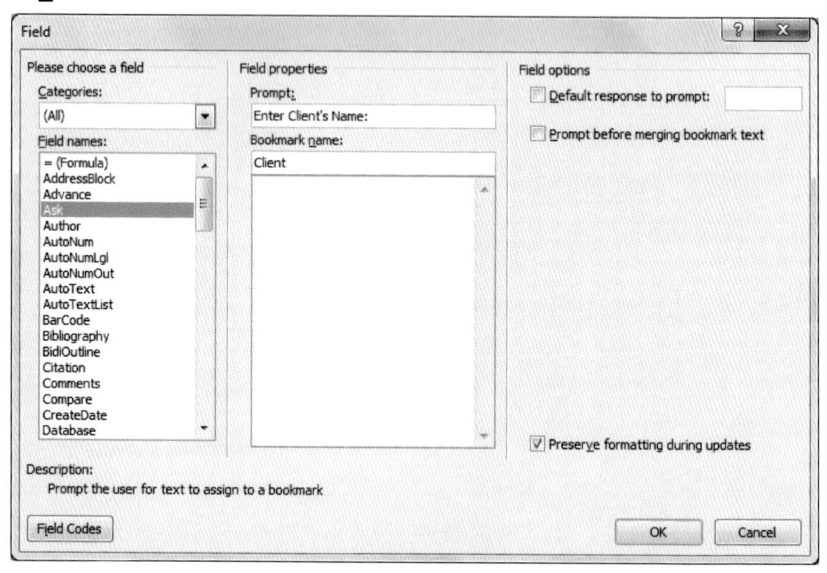

Figure 187

4. In Prompt: type, Enter Client's Name
5. In Bookmark name type Client, select Field Codes
6. Click OK, the following prompt appears

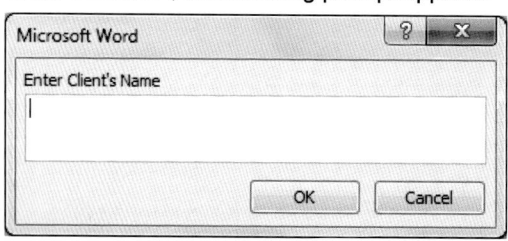

Figure 188

7. In the Enter Client's Name box type, ABC Limited, press OK

8. Type the following paragraph starting, This contract.....

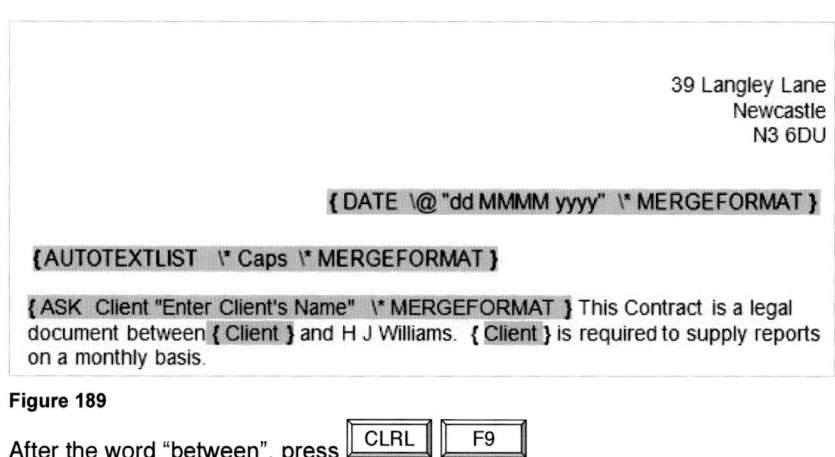

> 39 Langley Lane
> Newcastle
> N3 6DU
>
> { DATE \@ "dd MMMM yyyy" * MERGEFORMAT }
>
> {AUTOTEXTLIST * Caps * MERGEFORMAT }
>
> { ASK Client "Enter Client's Name" * MERGEFORMAT } This Contract is a legal document between { Client } and H J Williams. { Client } is required to supply reports on a monthly basis.

Figure 189

9. After the word "between", press `CLRL` `F9`
10. Type Client between the brackets as above
11. Repeat the process as shown above after the first sentence
12. Select `CTRL` `A` to highlight the whole document, press `F9`
13. The Enter Client's Name dialog box appears

Microsoft Word

Enter Client's Name
ABC Limited

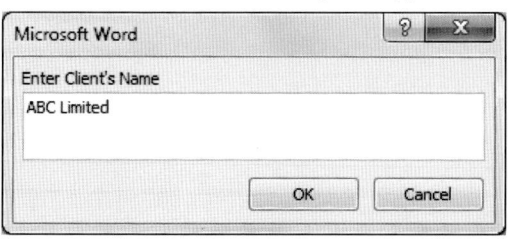

OK   Cancel

Figure 190

14. Click `OK`, press `ALT` `F9` to view the text on screen

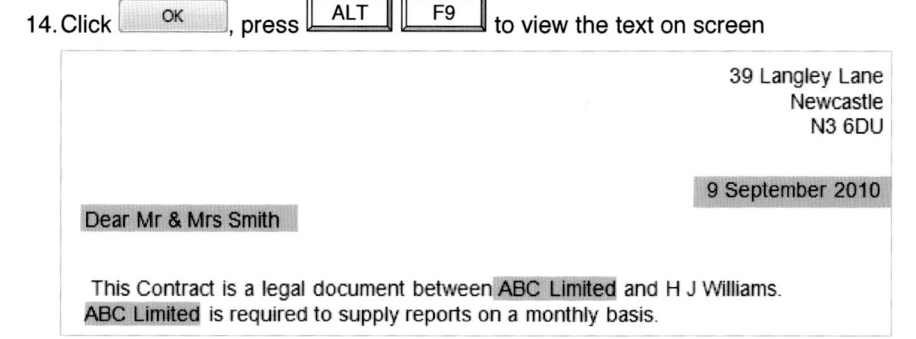

> 39 Langley Lane
> Newcastle
> N3 6DU
>
> 9 September 2010
>
> Dear Mr & Mrs Smith
>
> This Contract is a legal document between ABC Limited and H J Williams. ABC Limited is required to supply reports on a monthly basis.

Figure 191

15. Preview and save the document

Exercise 15: - Fill-in Fields

The Fill-in Field requires the user to input information at a particular location in the document where the field has been created.

1. Open the document used in the previous section
2. Select `Insert`, `Header`, centre align the header
3. Select `Insert`, `Quick Parts`, `Field...`
4. In **F**ield names: choose Fill-in

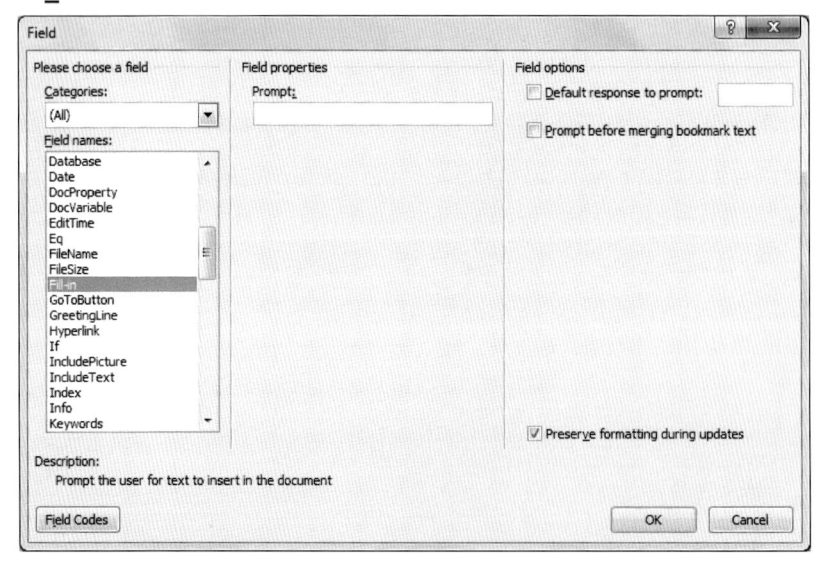

5. In the Prompt: field; type "Enter the company name"
6. Select `Field Codes`

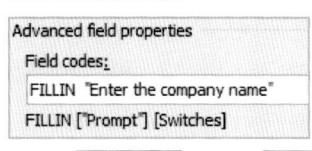

    Advanced field properties
    Field codes:
    FILLIN "Enter the company name"
    FILLIN ["Prompt"] [Switches]

7. Press `Hide Codes`, press `OK`

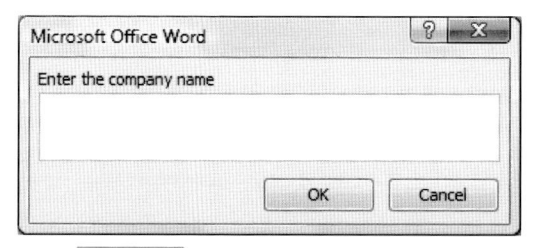

8. Click **OK**, the Fill-in field is displayed

   { FILLIN "Enter the company name" * MERGEFORMAT }

9. Create Fill-in fields for:

   { FILLIN "What position do you hold in the company?" * MERGEFORMAT }

   { FILLIN "What is your telephone number?" * MERGEFORMAT }

10. Create a closing using AutoText
11. Select **ALT** + **F9** to view the text
12. Save the document as a template, close the document
13. Create a new document based on the created template
14. Complete the Fill-in Fields as appropriate
15. Select **ALT** + **F9** to display the text
16. Preview and save the document

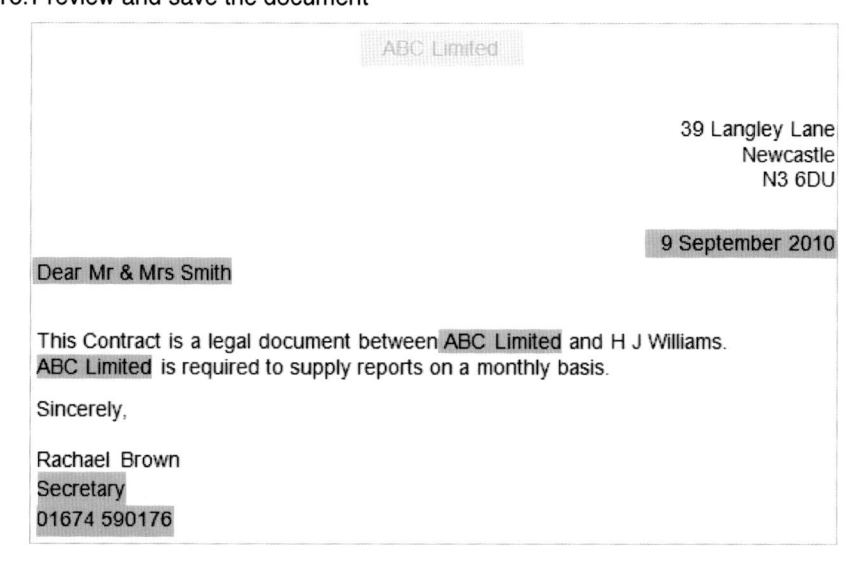

ABC Limited

39 Langley Lane
Newcastle
N3 6DU

9 September 2010

Dear Mr & Mrs Smith

This Contract is a legal document between ABC Limited and H J Williams. ABC Limited is required to supply reports on a monthly basis.

Sincerely,

Rachael Brown
Secretary
01674 590176

Macros

A macro allows the user to perform repeated tasks that combine multiple commands and automates complex tasks. Macros can be assigned to a specific document or generated from a template. Before recording a Macro prepare, plan and practice the steps to ensure that the commands function correctly.

Record a Macro

1. Open a new document
2. Select `View`, `Macros`, `Record Macro...`
3. Alternatively press `ALT` `W` `M` `R`
4. The Record Macro dialog box appears

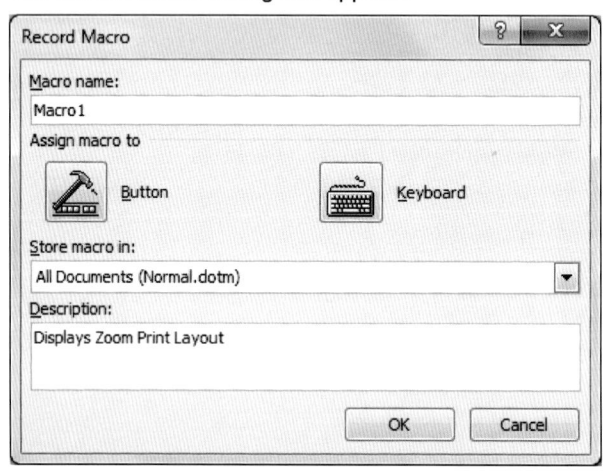

Figure 192

5. Complete the dialog box as shown above
6. Click the left button to assign the macro to the keyboard
7. The Customise Keyboard dialog box appears

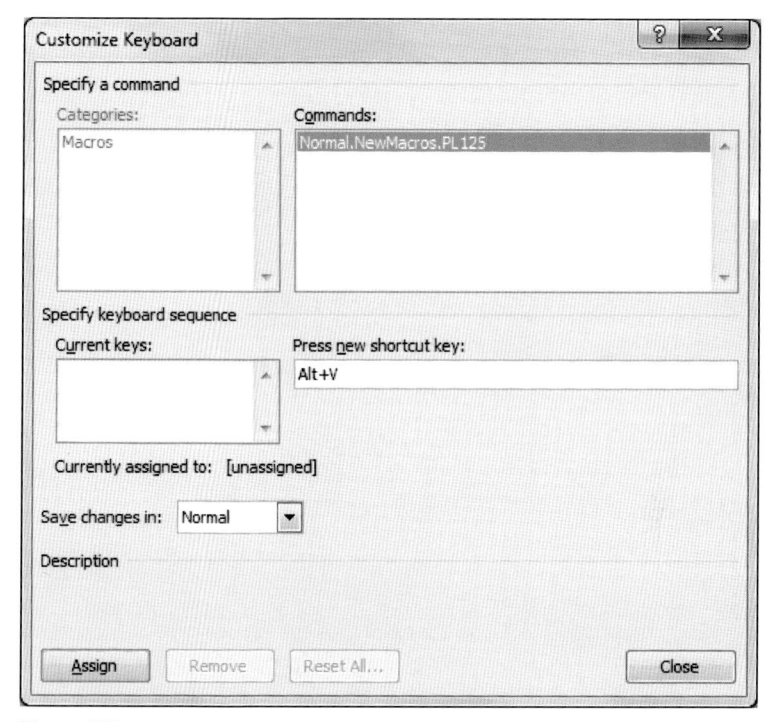

Figure 193

8. The flashing cursor appears in the press new shortcut key area
9. Hold down **ALT** and press **V**, the **Alt+V** states currently [unassigned]
10. Click **Assign**, press **Close**
11. Back in the document the mouse pointer has a tape icon attached
12. The status of the macro is recording
13. Click on the **Zoom** icon to display the zoom dialog box

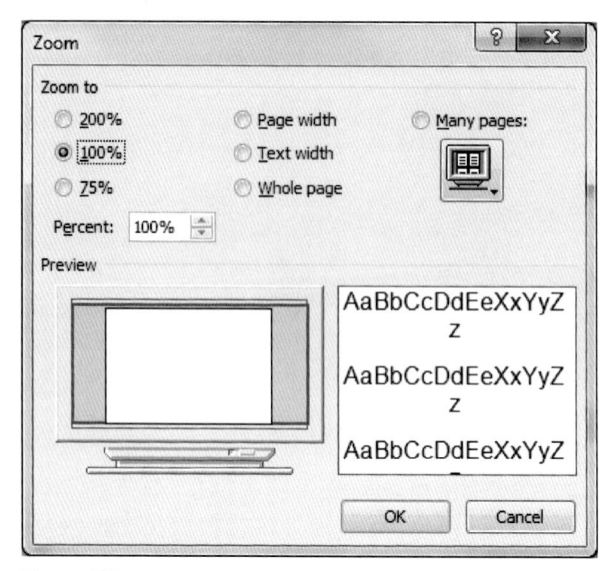

Figure 194

14. Type 125 in the `Percent: 125%` area or use the arrow keys to increase the percentage

15. Select `OK`, the page is zoomed to 125%

16. Click the left button in the Status Bar on the Stop Recording icon
`A macro is currently recording. Click to stop recording.`

17. Alternatively select `View`, `Macros`, `Stop Recording`

View and Edit a Macro

1. Select View , Macros, View Macros
2. Alternatively ALT F8 to display the Macros dialog box

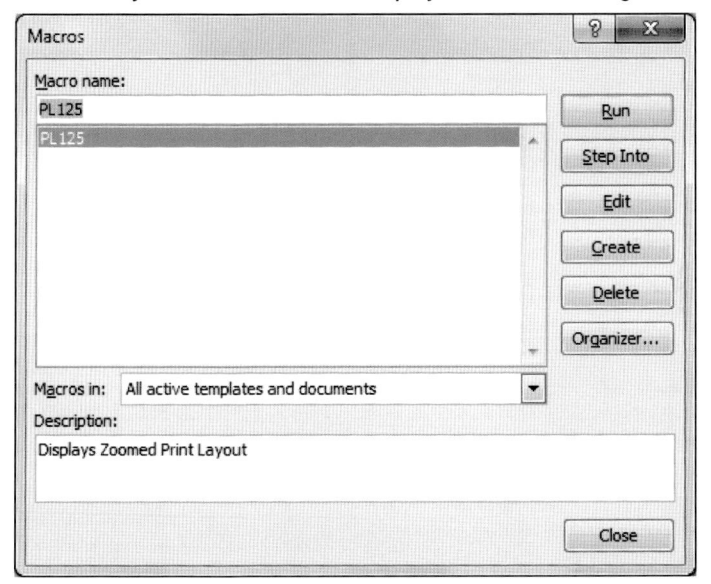

Figure 195

3. Click on PL125, select Edit
4. The Normal - NewMacros (Code) screen appears

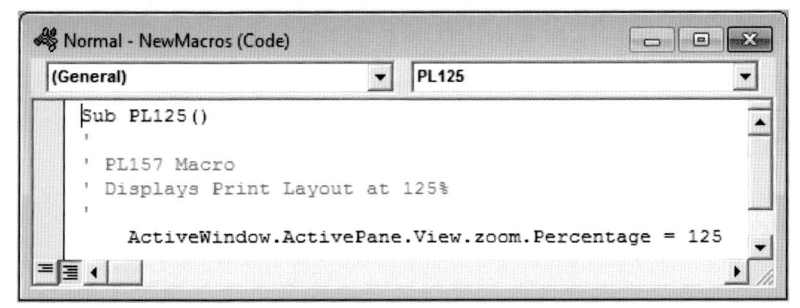

```
Sub PL125()

' PL157 Macro
' Displays Print Layout at 125%

    ActiveWindow.ActivePane.View.zoom.Percentage = 125
```

Figure 196

5. Ensure the cursor is placed at the beginning of the macro
6. Press CTRL F, the Find dialog box appears

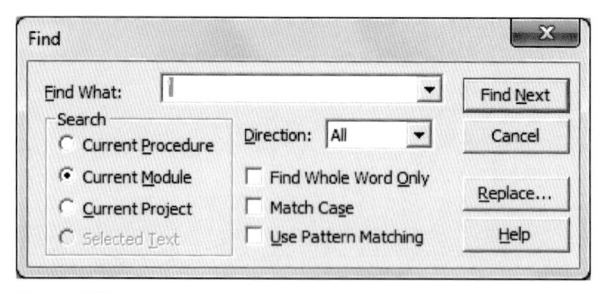

Figure 197

7. In the **F**ind What area, type 125, click on [Find Next] to find where 125 appears in the macro

8. Click [Replace] to display the Replace dialog box

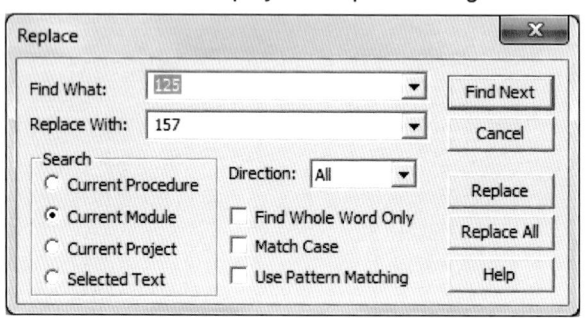

Figure 198

9. In the Find What: box type 125
10. In the Replace With: box type 157
11. Click [Replace], the macro is updated
12. Select [Replace] to find the next location in the macro to be updated
13. The following dialog box appears when all the locations have been updated

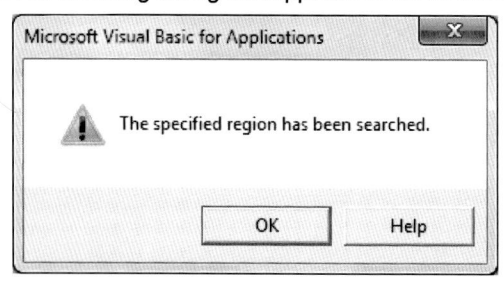

Figure 199

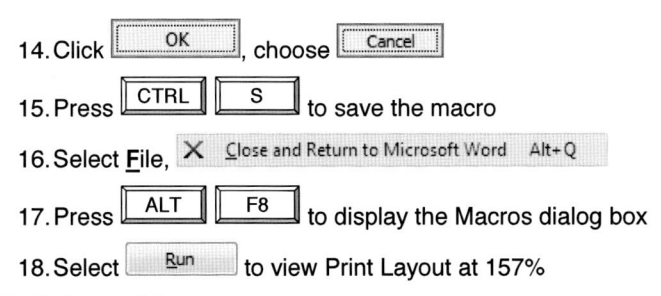

14. Click `OK`, choose `Cancel`
15. Press `CTRL` `S` to save the macro
16. Select File, × Close and Return to Microsoft Word Alt+Q
17. Press `ALT` `F8` to display the Macros dialog box
18. Select `Run` to view Print Layout at 157%

Deleting a Macro

1. Open the document that contains the macro to be deleted
2. Select `View`, `Macros`, `View Macros`

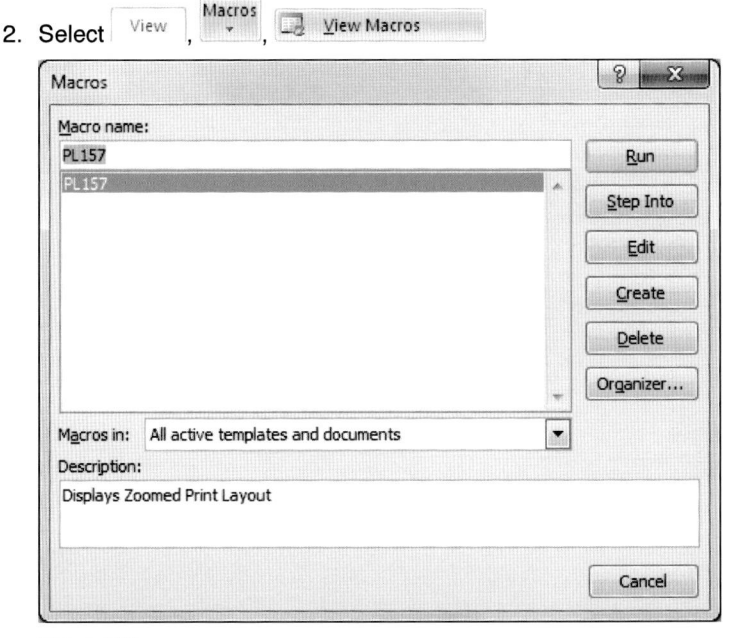

Figure 200

3. Press `Delete`

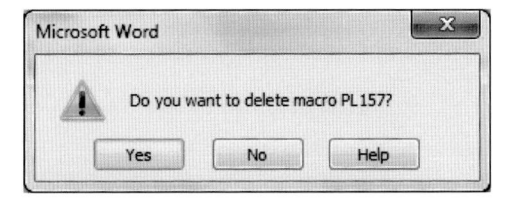

Figure 201

4. Select `Yes`, press `Close`

Exercise 16: - Generate a Table of Contents Macro

Table of Contents

Monday	2
Briefing at 10:00	2
Tuesday	3
Performance Review at 15:00	3
Wednesday	4
Progress Meeting 09:30	4
Thursday	5
Staff Appraisal at 14:15	5
Friday	6
Company Car New Criteria	6

1. Open a new document
2. Generate the Table of Contents above using Styles Heading 1-3
3. Change the Progress Meeting to 10:00
4. Save the document
5. Create a Macro to Update the Table of Contents
6. Preview the results

Watermarks

A watermark is any graphic or text that appears either on top or behind existing text when the document is printed, for example "Sample Document".

Picture Watermarks

1. Open a new document
2. Select `Page Layout`, `Watermark`, `Custom Watermark...`
3. Alternatively press `ALT` `P` `P` `W` `W`
4. The Printed Watermark dialog box appears
5. Select Picture watermark

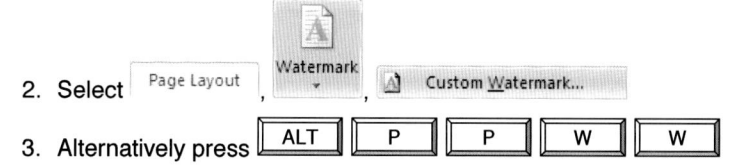

Figure 202

6. Choose `Select Picture...`, locate the picture, click `Insert`
7. Click `Apply`, choose `Close`
8. The watermark appears in the document
9. Preview the document to view the watermark

Text Watermark

1. Open a new document
2. Select `Page Layout`, `Watermark`, `Custom Watermark...`
3. Alternatively press `ALT` `P` `P` `W`
4. Choose the text required from the default settings

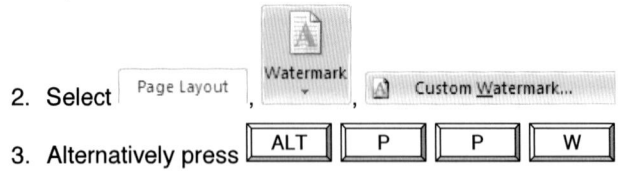

Figure 203

5. The watermark appears in the document

Customise a Text Watermark

1. Select `Page Layout`, `Watermark`, `Custom Watermark...`
2. The Printed Watermark dialog box appears

Figure 204

3. Select Te**x**t watermark, click on the ▼ arrow, select the required text

```
ASAP
CONFIDENTIAL
COPY
DO NOT COPY
DRAFT
ORIGINAL
```

Figure 205

4. Make changes to the **F**ont, **S**ize and **C**olour text layout as necessary
5. Click `Apply`, choose `Close`

Delete a Watermark

1. Select `Page Layout`, `Watermark`, `Remove Watermark`
2. The Watermark is removed from the document
3. Alternatively press `ALT` `P` `P` `W` `R`

Exercise 17: - Creating a Watermark

1. Create a Watermark
2. Edit the Watermark
3. Preview the Watermark
4. Delete the Watermark

Hyperlinks

Hyperlinks allow users to move to a new destination by clicking with the left button, for example using hyperlinks in an electronic document such as a Table of Contents where the mouse pointer is moved over the page number relating to a topic. Hyperlinks can contain links in the same document or links to other applications, or a particular website. Hyperlinks can be assigned to text, graphics or pictures and can be created to open an existing file, web page, a place in a document, create a link to a new document or an E-mail address.

Creating a Hyperlink to a Web Page

1. Open a new document, type Smart PC Guides
2. Click `Insert`, **Hyperlink**, alternatively press `CTRL` `K`
3. The Insert Hyperlink dialog box appears

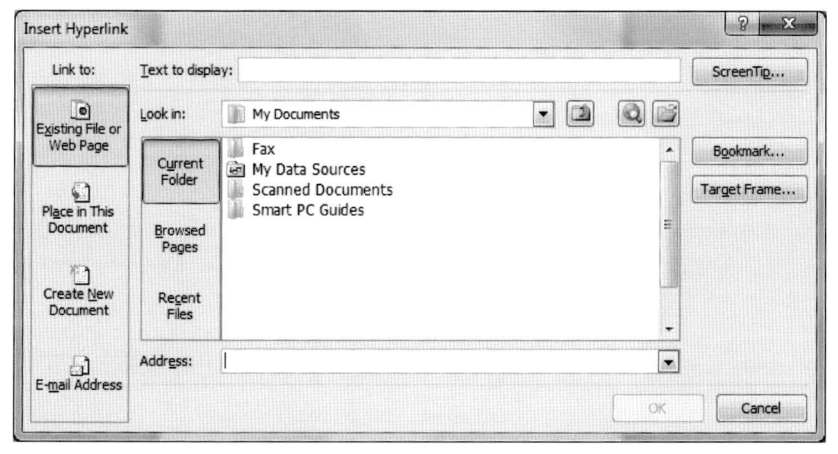

Figure 206

4. Under Link to: select E**x**isting File or Web Page
5. In the Add**r**ess field type the web address http://www.smart-pc-guides.com

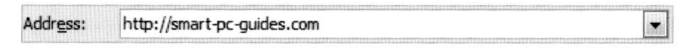

Figure 207

6. In the **T**ext to display area type Smart PC Guides, press `OK`
7. The hyperlink Smart PC Guides appears in the document
8. Hold the `CTRL` key down, click on the link with the left button
9. The Smart PC Guides Home Page appears
10. Click on the [X] to close the web page

Edit a Hyperlink

1. Press with the left 🖱 button on the hyperlink
2. Click with the right 🖱 button, select Edit <u>H</u>yperlink

Figure 208

3. The Edit Hyperlink dialog box appears

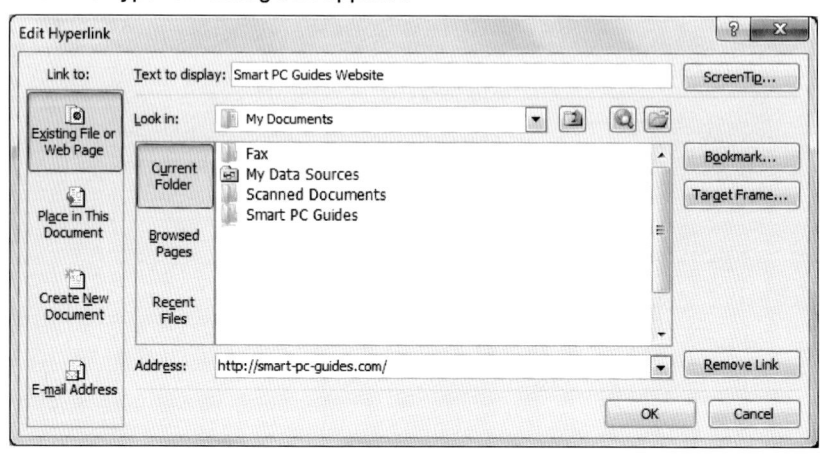

Figure 209

4. In <u>T</u>ext to display, change the information as shown above, click **OK**
5. The new link is displayed as Smart PC Guides Website

Delete a Hyperlink

1. Select the Hyperlink Smart PC Guides Website
2. Click with the right 🖱 button, select ❌ Remove Hyperlink
3. The text is displayed without the hyperlink

Creating a Hyperlink in a Document

1. Create a bookmark within a document, for example Chapter 1
2. Repeat the process to create bookmarks for Chapters 2 and 3
3. Select the position where you want to create a hyperlink
4. Click Insert, Hyperlink, alternatively press CTRL K
5. The Insert Hyperlink dialog box appears
6. Select Place in This Document

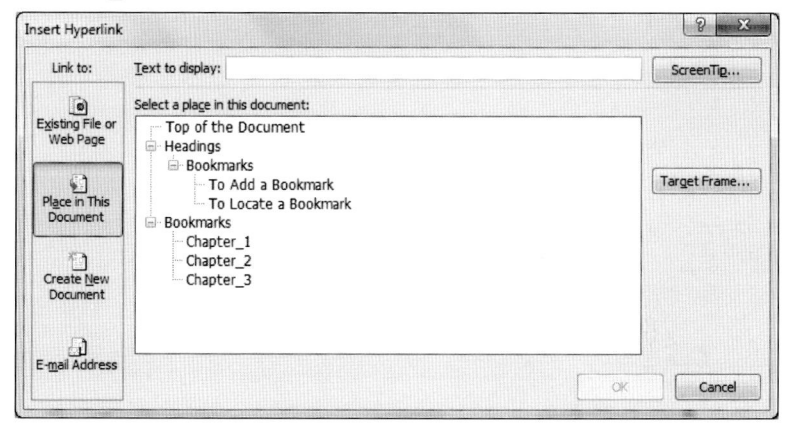

Figure 210

7. Choose the bookmark Chapter_1, select OK
8. Press the CTRL key, click on the link with the left 🖱 button
9. The cursor appears before the text Chapter 1

Columns Feature

1. Open a new document
2. Choose `Page Layout`, `Breaks` to expand the menu
3. Choose **Continuous** (Insert a section break and start the new section on the same page.)
4. Alternatively press `ALT` `I` `B`

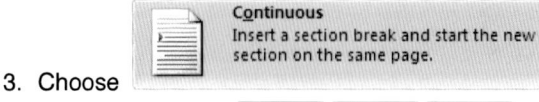

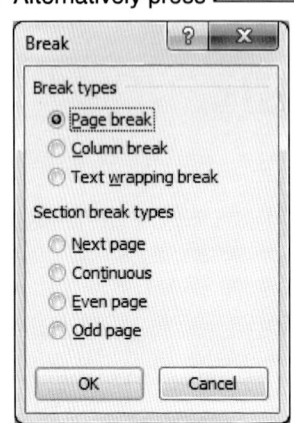

Figure 211

5. Choose `Continuous`, press `OK`
6. Select `Page Layout`, `Columns` to expand the menu
7. Choose `More Columns...` to display the Columns dialog box
8. Alternatively press `ALT` `O` `C`

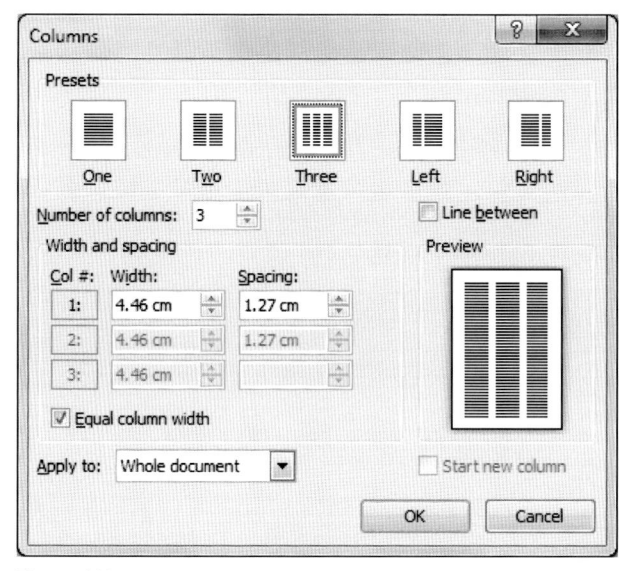

Figure 212

9. Select Pre-sets, choose **T**hree
10. The Preview area displays the chosen selection
11. W**i**dth and **S**pacing can be adjusted using the arrows
12. Select **A**pply to, choose This point forward

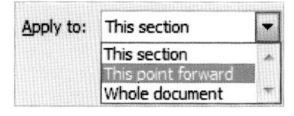

Figure 213

13. click OK, type the required text or copy and paste the text
14. The text appears in the columns
15. To return to a single column, choose Page Layout, Breaks
16. Choose Continuous – Insert a section break and start the new section on the same page.
17. Press ALT O C to display the Columns dialog box
18. Select One
19. Select **A**pply to, choose This point forward, click OK

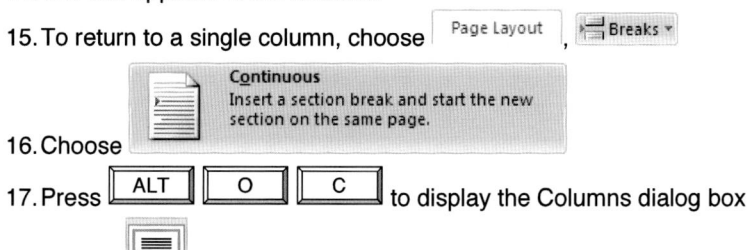

Charts

Insert a Chart in a Document

1. Position the cursor where the chart is required
2. Select `Insert`, `Object`
3. The Object dialog box appears

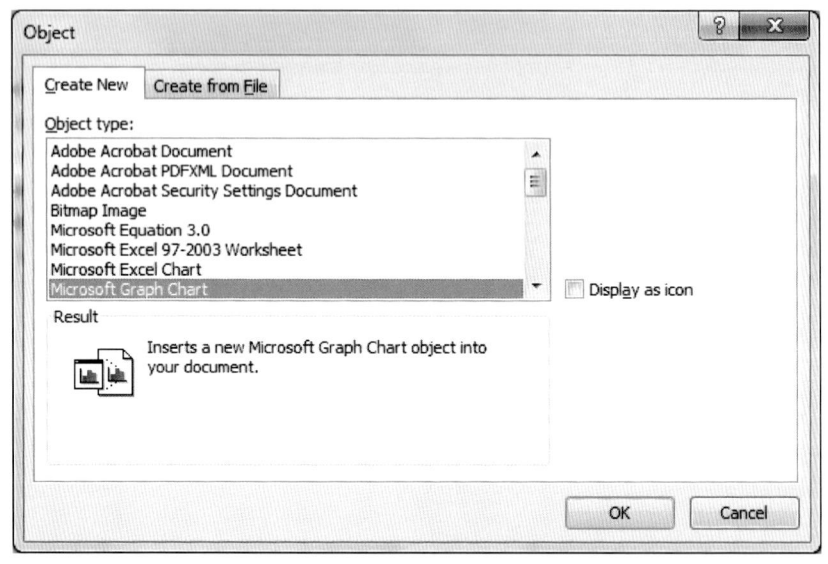

Figure 214

4. Choose <u>C</u>reate New, arrow down and select Microsoft Graph Chart
5. Click `OK`, the Datasheet box appears showing the default chart

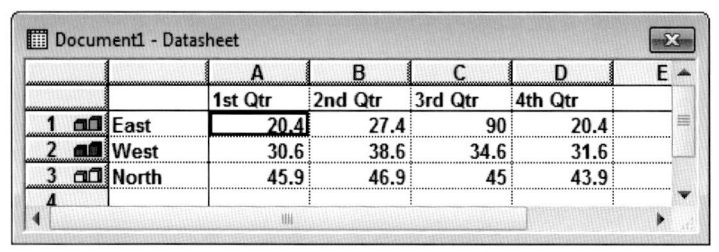

		A	B	C	D	E
		1st Qtr	2nd Qtr	3rd Qtr	4th Qtr	
1	East	20.4	27.4	90	20.4	
2	West	30.6	38.6	34.6	31.6	
3	North	45.9	46.9	45	43.9	
4						

Figure 215

6. To adjust columns or rows, click on the sizing handles and drag
7. Delete the existing text in the default datasheet
8. To alter text or figures, click in a cell and type the required text
9. Click outside the document, the chart appears in the document

Edit a Chart

1. Double click the left 🖱 button in the chart to bring up the datasheet
2. Amend the text as required, click outside the document
3. The amended chart is displayed in the document

Copy Information from Excel

1. Open Microsoft Excel, create the following data in a new spreadsheet

	A	B
1		Sales
2	January	£12,437.00
3	February	£13,478.00
4	March	£23,994.00
5	April	£9,854.00
6	May	£15,890.00
7	June	£30,125.00

Figure 216

2. Click the left 🖱 button in cell A1, highlight to B7
3. Select CTRL C
4. Switch to Microsoft Word
5. Press the left 🖱 button where the data is to appear
6. Select CTRL V to paste the information into the document

Paste Special

1. Highlight the cells in Excel to be copied to Word
2. Return to the Word document
3. Choose Home , Paste , Paste Special...
4. Alternatively ALT CTRL V displays the Paste Special dialog box
5. Select the option Paste link
6. Choose Microsoft Office Excel Worksheet Object

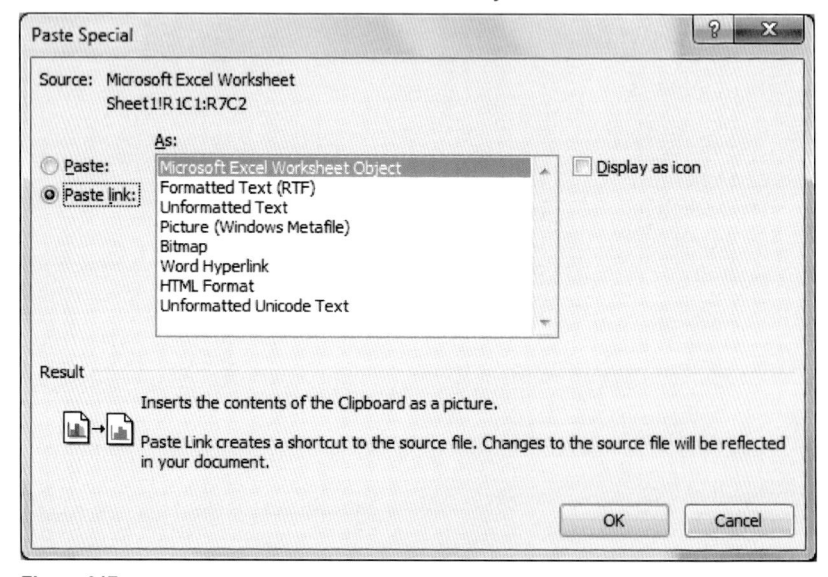

Figure 217

7. Click OK to paste the link into the document

	Sales
January	£12,437.00
February	£13,478.00
March	£23,994.00
April	£9,854.00
May	£15,890.00
June	£30,125.00

Figure 218

8. Change the information in one cell in Excel, switch back to Word
9. The Word document has been updated

Note: Make sure that the user has access to all linked information if this option is used.

Exercise 18: - Columns, Hyperlinks and Macros

Using 2 columns read the following text; reproduce the exercise exactly as shown in a new blank document. Save the document as Mylinks.doc

- Open up a New blank document
- Save the document
- Name the document as Mylinks.doc

1. Select Format, Columns
2. Choose a two column option
3. Create the text as shown

Open Excel

- Open up Microsoft Excel
- Select a cell of your choice
- Create the information below
- Save the spreadsheet as linking.xls
- Close the spreadsheet

Month	Sales
January	£12,437.00
February	£13,478.00
March	£23,994.00
April	£9,854.00
May	£15,890.00
June	£30,125.00

Inserting Excel Data

1. Select the position to insert in Word
2. Click, Insert Object
3. Select the option, Create from File
4. Place a tick in the box, Link to File
5. Browse for the excel file required
6. Select OK
7. The data from Excel appears in Word

Note: If the link to file option is used any changes will affect the layout of this document e.g. if you created a chart in the same worksheet

Modify Linked Data

- Double click on the excel data
- Select the excel data
- Change the font size to Size 9
- Select Save in Excel
- Close Down Excel
- The data changes in the Document

Open Excel

1. Open the file in Excel named Linking
2. In the Month Column
3. Change months July to December
4. Save the Excel document

Inserting Excel Data

- Open an existing spreadsheet
- Highlight the text
- Select CTRL C
- Switch to Microsoft Word
- ALT CTRL V for Paste Special
- Select Paste the source as a picture
- Click OK
- The results appear in Word

Create a Macro

Create macro named **AutoExec** assign this to a document. The macro should go into preview upon opening. Create a second macro assigned to the same document only using the shortcut key ALT and E to close the document.

Using Hyperlinks in PowerPoint

Staff that deliver presentations might consider using hyperlinks, the benefit being that when delivering a presentation a hyperlink could enable the audience to view statistical information in either Word or Excel.

- Create a hyperlink
- Leave the text to display field blank
- Locate the required file
- Click on the OK icon

When running the slide show

- Move the mouse pointer over the slide
- Click with the left mouse button
- The file opens

To return back to the presentation, select ALT and E from the macro that was created in Word to close the file and returns the person back to the PowerPoint presentation.

Graphics

Documents can be enhanced and made more interesting by inserting graphics, drawing objects, pictures, charts or text. A Bitmap picture made up from a series of small dots that form shapes and lines cannot be converted to drawing objects or ungrouped but can be scaled, cropped and re-coloured. Pictures made up as metafiles (most ClipArt) can be ungrouped.

Inserting a Picture in a Document

1. Open a document where a picture is required
2. Place the cursor at the point where the picture is to be inserted
3. Select `Insert`, `Clip Art`, the Clip Art dialog box appears

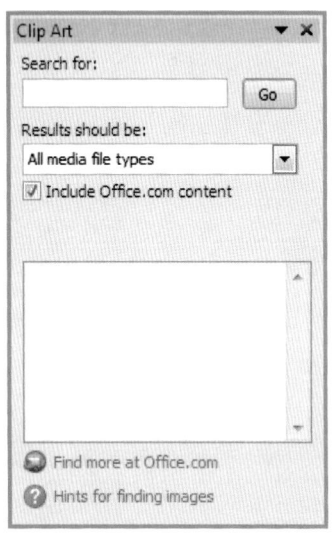

Figure 219

4. In the Search for: box type, Business, press `Go`
5. The Clip Art dialog box shows the results
6. Use the scroll bar to view the options
7. Click on the ▼ arrow on the picture, select `Insert`

Figure 220

8. The picture is displayed in the document
9. To delete the picture, click in the picture with the left button
10. Press [Delete]

Edit a Picture in a Document

1. Open a document that contains text and a picture, click on the picture

Figure 221

2. Move the mouse pointer over the sizing handles, drag to edit the picture
3. To move the picture to another position, click in the picture and drag
4. To rotate the picture, click in the picture, the Picture Tools Format Tab appears
5. Select Format, choose Rotate from the Format Arrange Grouping
6. Move the mouse pointer over the options to show how the picture looks

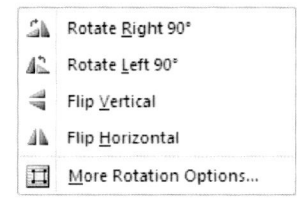

- Rotate Right 90°
- Rotate Left 90°
- Flip Vertical
- Flip Horizontal
- More Rotation Options...

Figure 222

7. Select Flip Horizontal
8. Move the mouse pointer to a green circle, a black circular arrow appears
9. Click and hold down the left button drag to rotate to the required position

Figure 223

Cropping Pictures

The Picture Tools option appears when a picture is selected in a document.

1. Click the left button on the **Format** Tab to display the Picture Tools
2. Select a picture by using the left button

Figure 224

3. Click the Crop icon from the Picture Tools

Figure 225

4. Move over a black handle
5. Drag over the area that needs to be taken out
6. Repeat the process until you see the tiger's face

Figure 226

7. Press the left button and drag to hide the information not required
8. Select Size from the **Format** Tab

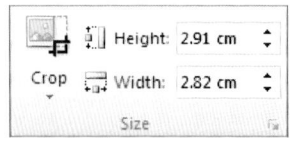

Figure 227

9. Click the arrows in the height and width area to increase or decrease the size
10. Expand the Size Grouping by clicking on , the Layout dialog box appears

11. Ensure the Size Tab is selected
12. Alternatively select the picture to be resized
13. Right click on the picture select Size and Position...

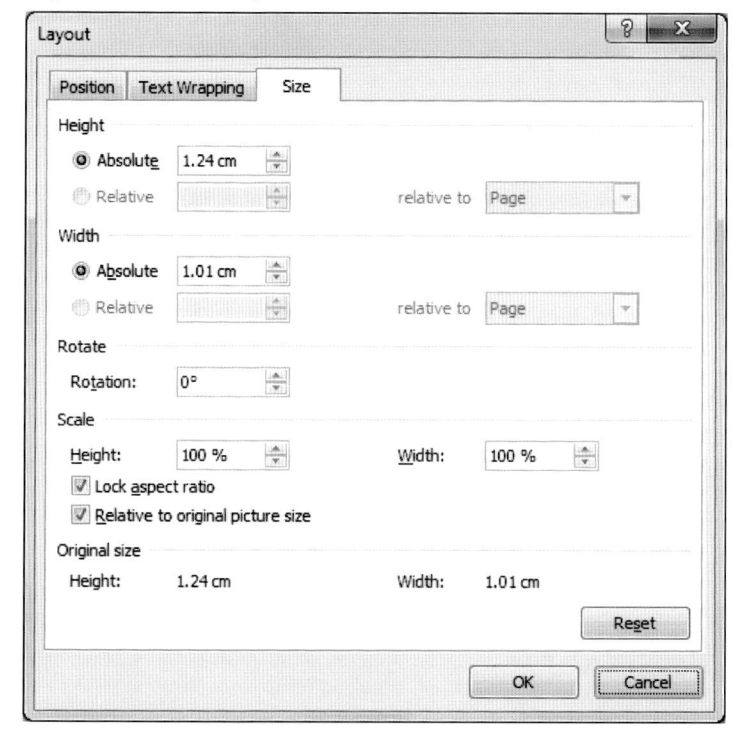

Figure 228

14. In the Scale area, amend the **H**eight and **W**idth to 300%
15. Click OK

Inserting WordArt into a Document

1. To insert text as an object, select Insert, WordArt
2. The WordArt Gallery appears

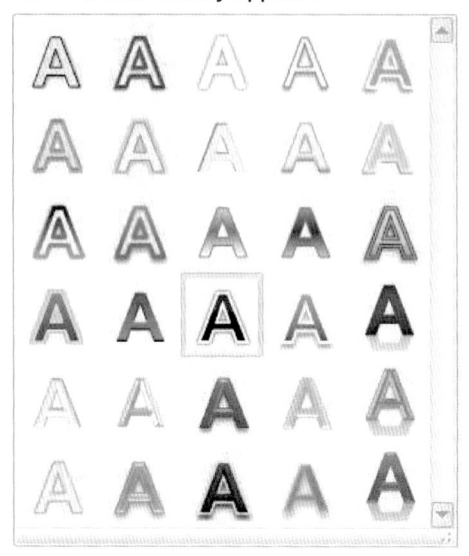

Figure 229

3. Select a style to appear in the document

Figure 230

4. Type the required text

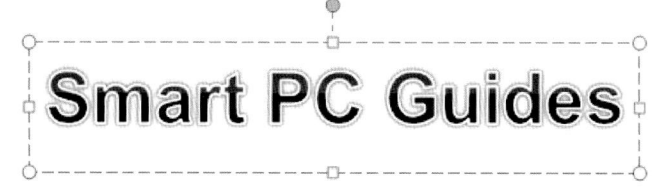

Figure 231

5. The Drawing Tools Tab appears **Format** in the Ribbon
6. Click on **Text Effects** in the WordArt Styles Grouping
7. Choose **3-D Rotation**, select Perspective Right

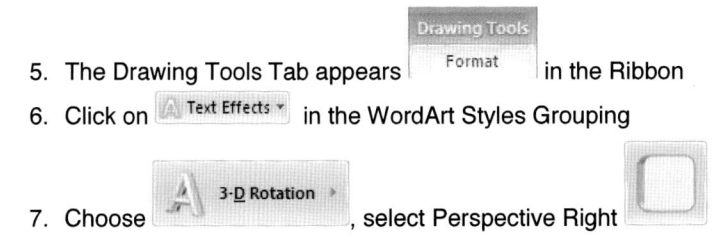

Smart PC Guides

Figure 232

Adding Shadows

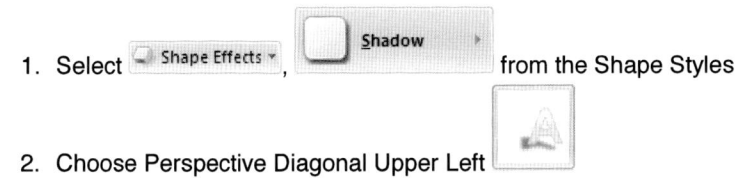

1. Select **Shape Effects**, **Shadow** from the Shape Styles
2. Choose Perspective Diagonal Upper Left

Smart PC Guides

Figure 233

Edit WordArt in a Document

1. Click with the left button on the text to be edited
2. Edit text as required

Formatting WordArt in a Document

1. To change the colour of the WordArt, select the text to be changed
2. Click **Text Fill**, choose the required colour

Smart PC Guides

Figure 234

Adding AutoShapes to Documents

Ready-made basic shapes, for example rectangles, circles, block arrows, flowcharts, symbols, banners and callouts can be added to documents to enhance its appearance.

1. Select `Insert`, **Shapes** from the Illustrations grouping
2. The Shapes gallery appears, choose Callouts

Figure 235

3. Select a shape

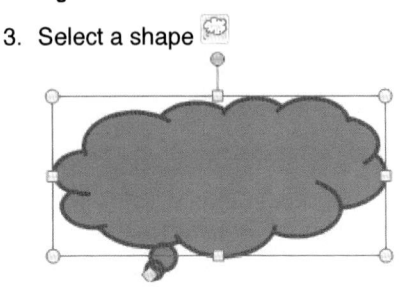

Figure 236

4. Drag in the document for the AutoShape to appear
5. Type the text required in the AutoShape
6. The text appears in the AutoShape in the document

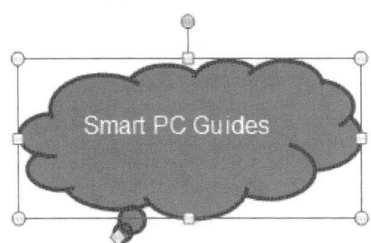

Figure 237

7. Click the downward arrow to reveal more options

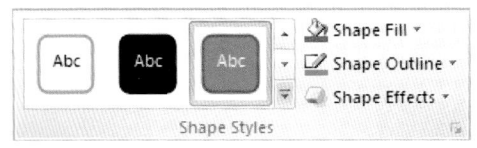

Figure 238

8. Select Intense Effect, Orange, Accent 6

Figure 239

Drawing Tools

1. To use a drawing object, select Line from the Shapes gallery

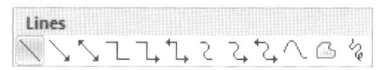

Figure 240

2. Hold down the left button and drag
3. Click back on the Line icon
4. Position the mouse pointer on the circle next to the line and drag

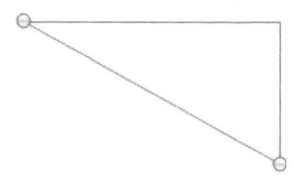

Figure 241

5. Repeat the above steps to complete the required shape
6. To draw a shape, click on the shape from the Shapes gallery
7. Move the mouse pointer where the object is to appear
8. Hold down the left button and drag, release the mouse button
9. Repeat the process to create as many shapes as required

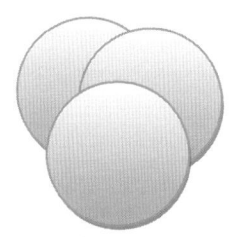

Figure 242

Drawing Objects

1. Click in the document where the object is to appear
2. Select an object from the Shapes gallery using the left [mouse] button
3. Press and hold down the [Shift] key, drag the object onto the page
4. Release the mouse button before the [Shift] key
5. Click outside the drawing box

Figure 243

6. To add a 3-D effect, select the object
7. Select [Format] from the Drawing Tools Tab
8. Click on [Shape Effects ▾], [Preset ▸], choose Pre-set 9

Figure 244

9. To format the 3-D Shape,
10. Select [Shape Effects ▾], [Preset ▸], [3-D Options...]
11. The Format Shape dialog box appears
12. Click [Close] to return to the document

Text Boxes

Text boxes allow text to be positioned anywhere in a document.

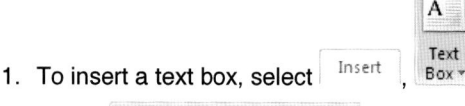

1. To insert a text box, select Insert , Text Box ▼
2. Select Draw Text Box
3. Click where you want to start the text box, drag to the required size

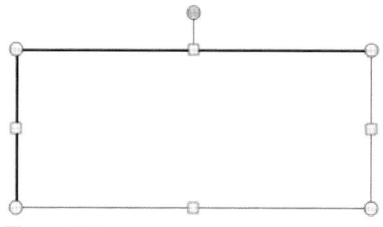

Figure 245

4. Type inside the box to add text
5. To move the text box, click on the edge of the box
6. Use the arrow keys ↓ ↑ → ← to move the text box to the new position
7. Alternatively click with the left button on the edge of the text box and drag
8. Release the mouse when the text box is in its new location
9. To delete a box, position the mouse pointer over the edge of the text box
10. A four headed arrow appears, click on the border, press Delete
11. Alternatively click with the left button on the edge of the text box and drag
12. Release the mouse when the text box is in its new location
13. To delete a box, position the mouse pointer over the edge of the text box
14. A four headed arrow appears, click on the border, press Delete

Linking Text Boxes

Linking allows text to flow from one text box to another.

1. Select the text boxes where text is to flow from
2. Select **Create Link** from the **Format** Tab (Drawing Tools)
3. Position the cursor over the second text box
4. Click with the left button the Mug pointer is displayed with an arrow
5. Type the text in the first box
6. The text automatically flows into the second text box

Display Text Box Tools

When a text box is selected, text box tools is displayed enabling the user to change features using Groups and Commands that relate to drawing, changing text direction, creating and breaking linked text boxes, text box styles, shadow effects, 3D effects, arranging and positioning text boxes and changing the size of text boxes.

Text Wrapping

Text can be forced to wrap around objects in a document.

1. Open a new document
2. Type the text shown below

    By moving the wrap points the text wraps around the butterfly so that the butterfly sits nicely inside the text and so becomes part of the text

    Figure 246

3. Select a place in the text where the picture is to appear
4. **Insert**, **Clip Art**
5. The Clip Art dialog box appears
6. In the Search for: box type butterfly, press **Go**
7. The Clip Art dialog box shows the results

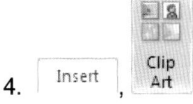

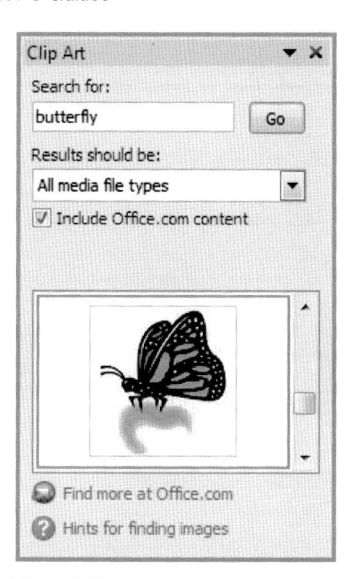

Figure 247

8. Double click on the required picture to insert it

Figure 248

9. Right click on the picture
10. Select **Group**, **Ungroup**
11. The following dialog box appears

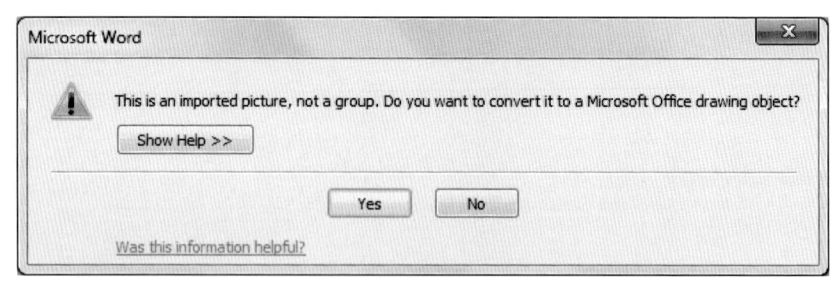

Figure 249

12. Select [Yes], a canvas is inserted around the picture

Figure 250

13. Click with the left 🖱 button on the canvas border
14. Drag to the required position over the text
15. Right 🖱 click on the canvas border
16. Choose Wrap Text   ▶ ,   Edit Wrap Points

By moving the wrap the butterfly so that the text and so becomes part

points the text wraps around butterfly sits nicely inside the of the text

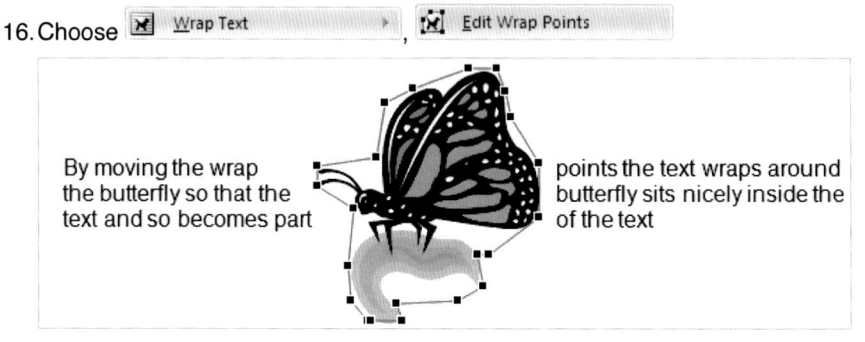

Figure 251

17. Click on the black squares and drag to the required position

18. The text appears around the picture

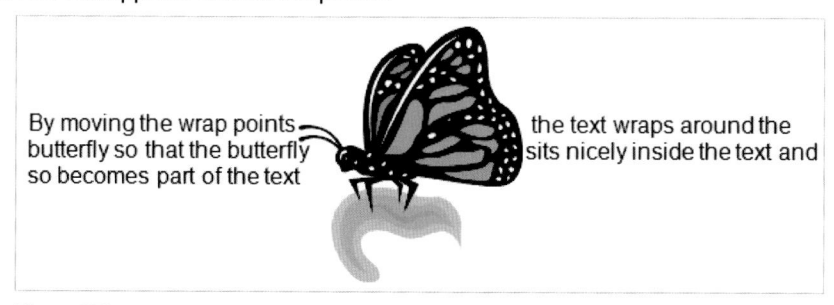

By moving the wrap points butterfly so that the butterfly so becomes part of the text the text wraps around the sits nicely inside the text and

Figure 252

19. To regroup the picture, click with the left button on the canvas border
20. Select CTRL A
21. Click with the right button, select Group , Group

Footnotes and Endnotes

A footnote explains what text is in a document and is placed at the foot of a page. If it is placed at the end of the document it is known as an Endnote. Footnotes and Endnotes consist of two parts, the note reference mark that is characterised by a number or character within the body of the text referring to additional text in a footnote, and the note text that contains the descriptive text.

Inserting a Footnote

1. Position the pointer in the text where the footnote reference mark is to appear
2. Select, References, Insert Footnote
3. The following prompt appears at the foot of the page

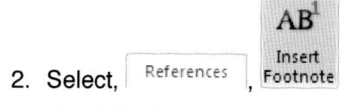

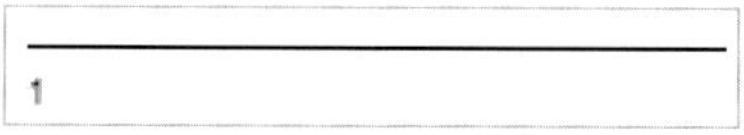

1

Figure 253

4. Type the text required for the footnote
5. The following prompt appears in the document to indicate a footnote [1]

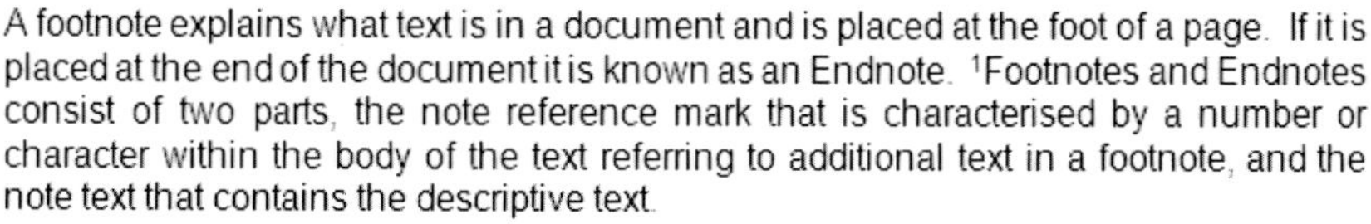

   A footnote explains what text is in a document and is placed at the foot of a page. If it is placed at the end of the document it is known as an Endnote. [1]Footnotes and Endnotes consist of two parts, the note reference mark that is characterised by a number or character within the body of the text referring to additional text in a footnote, and the note text that contains the descriptive text.

Figure 254

6. The note text appears at the bottom of the page

> ¹ The note appears at the foot of the page

Figure 255

Inserting a Endnote

Follow the steps for Footnote, select [Insert Endnote]

1. The endnote reference mark appears in the text identified by an ⁱ
2. The endnote appears at the end of the document

> ¹ This endnote appears at the end of the document

Figure 256

Amending a Footnote or Endnote

1. Move the mouse pointer over the footnote or endnote reference mark in the text
2. Double click with the left button
3. The cursor appears at the end of the page, amend text as necessary
4. Click with the left button to take you back to the document

Deleting a Footnote or Endnote

Place the mouse pointer over the footnote or endnote reference mark in the text, press [Delete]

Renumbering a Footnote or Endnote

1. Select [References], click on the downward pointing arrow from the Footnotes grouping

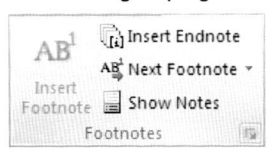

Figure 257

2. The Footnote and Endnote dialog appears

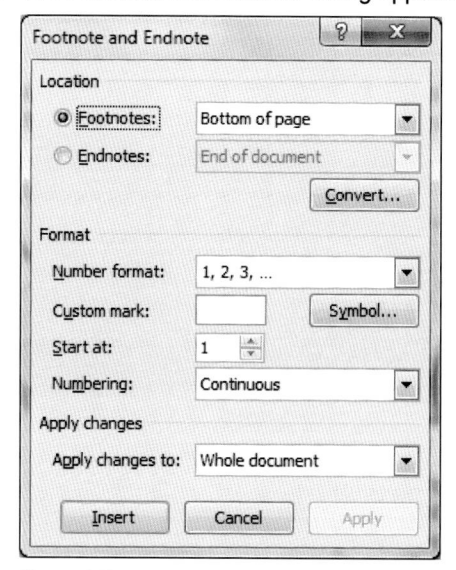

Figure 258

3. Select Footnotes, choose Numbering

Click Restart each page [Restart each page], press [Apply]

This concludes the Word 2010 Foundation to Expert Guide. Thank you for choosing Smart PC Guides. To see the complete range of Smart PC Guides please visit our website www.smart-pc-guides.com

Shortcut Keys

SHORTCUT KEYS	DESCRIPTION	SHORTCUT KEYS	DESCRIPTION
CTRL F1	Hide or Display the Ribbon	F1	Help
CTRL F2	Displays Print Preview	F5	Go To Dialog Box
CTRL A	Highlights Whole Document	F7	Spell Checker
CTRL B	Apply /Remove Bold Format	F10	Display/Hide Shortcut Keys
CTRL C	Copy Text	F12	Save As Dialog Box
CTRL D	Displays Font Dialog Box	ALT F8	Displays Macro Dialog Box
CTRL E	Centre Alignment	SHIFT F3	Caps/Lower/Title Case
CTRL F	Find	SHIFT F7	Thesaurus Feature
CTRL G	Displays Go To Dialog Box	ALT F T	Word Options Dialog Box
CTRL H	Displays Find and Replace Box	ALT I B	Insert Break
CTRL I	Apply/Remove Text in Italic	ALT N K	Bookmark Dialog Box
CTRL J	Apply/ Remove Justification	ALT O C	Columns Dialog Box
CTRL L	Aligns Text to the Left	ALT O T	Tabs Dialog Box
CTRL N	Inserts New Document	ALT W E	Draft View
CTRL O	Displays Open Dialog Box	ALT W F	Full Screen Reading View
CTRL P	Displays Print Dialog Box	ALT W L	Web Layout View
CTRL R	Align Text to Right	ALT W P	Print Layout View
CTRL S	Saves the Document	ALT W R	Display/Hide Ruler
CTRL U	Apply/Remove Underline	ALT N T D	Draw Table Tool
CTRL V	Paste Information	ALT S T I	Table of Contents Dialog Box
CTRL X	Cuts Information	ALT P P W	Watermark
CTRL Y	Redo Feature	ALT P P W R	Removes Watermark
CTRL Z	Undo Feature	ALT W M R	Record Macro Dialog Box

Index

Accessibility Checker 126
Actions 30, 32
Ask Field 152
AutoCorrect Feature
   Deleting an AutoCorrect Entry 35
   Opening the AutoCorrect Feature 33
AutoFit Feature 59
AutoFormat Feature 59
Automatic Update Feature 78
AutoShapes 182
AutoText Entries 148
   Ask Field 152
   AutoText List 151
   Date Fields 150
AutoText List 151
Bibliography 92, 94, 98
Bookmarks
   Adding a Bookmark 84
   Deleting a Bookmark 86
   Locating a Bookmark 85
Breaks
   Create a Section Break 65
   Delete Page, Column or Section 68
Bulleted Lists 47, 51
Bullets and Numbering
   Bullet Library 47
   Bulleted Lists as you Type 47
   Continue a Numbered List 49
   Customised Bulleted List 48
   Numbered List 49
   Own Numbering Style 50
   Restart Numbering 49
Charts
   Edit a Chart 173
   Insert a Chart in a Document 172
Check Box Fields 141, 144
Citations 92, 95, 97
Columns 53, 54, 175
Columns Feature 170
Comments
   Deleting a Comment 101
   Editing a Comment 100
   Inserting a Comment 100
   Viewing Comments 101
Copy Information 28, 29, 173
Creating and Saving a Document 14
Cropping Pictures 178
Date Fields 150
Demote Information 131
Dictionary 25
Documents 13
Draft View 12
Drag and Copy Information 28
Drawing Pencil 62

Drawing Tools 183
Drives, Folders and Files 13
   Creating a Folder 14
   Creating a Sub-Folder 14
   Documents 13
Endnotes 189
Exercise 01
   Creating and Saving a Document 19
Exercise 02
   Copy and Move Functions 29
Exercise 03
   Add an Address to Actions 32
Exercise 04
   Bulleted Lists 51
Exercise 05
   Creating a Simple Table 57
Exercise 06
   Creating a Booking Form 64
Exercise 07
   Creating a Header and Footer 69
Exercise 08
   Creating Tabs 74
Exercise 09
   Creating a Document using Styles 83
Exercise 10
   Updating a Table of Contents 88
Exercise 11
   Add a Bibliography 98
Exercise 12
   Creating Labels 121
Exercise 13
   Working with a Table of Contents 133
Exercise 14
   Creating a Form 139
Exercise 15
   Fill-in Fields 154
Exercise 16
   Generate a Table of Contents Macro 162
Exercise 17
   Creating a Watermark 166
Exercise 18
   Columns, Hyperlinks and Macros 175
File Tab 10
   Adding Recently Used Documents 20
   Pin a Document to the Recent
      Docuemnt Area 21
Files 13
Fill-in Fields 154
Folders 13
Footnotes 189
Footnotes and Endnotes
   Amending a Footnote or Endnote 190
   Deleting a Footnote or Endnote 190
   Inserting an Endnote 190

Inserting a Footnote 189	View and Edit a Macro...................... 159
Renumbering a Footnote or Endnote 190	Mail Merge
Form Commands........................... 138, 139	Creating Labels using Mail Merge.... 114
Form Protection 146	Creating Letters using Mail Merge.... 104
Format Menu 37	Master Documents
Format Options 35	Creating a Master Document............ 135
Formatting Font Group 36	Delete a Subdocument 138
Keep Lines Together........................... 41	Inserting a Subdocument.................. 137
Keep with Next Option 41	Lock and Unlock Subdocuments...... 138
Menu Options 37	Moving a Subdocument..................... 138
Page Break Before 41	Opening a Subdocument................... 136
Paragraph Group.................................. 38	Merge Cells 54
Suppress Line Numbers...................... 41	Move Information 29
Text Wrap 41	Move,Drag and Drop Information 27
Widow/Orphan Control......................... 41	Moving Information 27
Format Painter... 41	Multiple Documents
Forms... 64	Compare & Combine Multiple Copies
Customising Check Box Form Fields 144	 101
Customising Text Form Fields 142	Navigation Pane....................................... 11
Inserting Check Box Form Fields...... 141	Numbered List.. 49
Inserting Text Form Fields 140	Objectives
Protecting Forms................................ 146	Expert Level.................................... 3, 129
Grammar Check Facility.......................... 25	Foundation Level 3, 9
Graphics	Intermediate Level 3, 58
Adding AutoShapes to Documents ... 182	Objects... 184
Adding Shadows 181	Opening Documents
Cropping Pictures............................... 178	Amend or Delete recently used Files . 23
Drawing Objects from a Central Point	File Tab 20
.... 184	Open Documents using the Mouse.... 21
Drawing Tools 183	Open Documents using the Shift Key 22
Edit a Picture in a Document............. 177	Open Documents with the Control Key
Editing WordArt in a Document......... 181	 22
Formatting WordArt in a Document .. 181	Opening Microsoft Word 13
Inserting a Picture in a Document..... 176	Outline View 12
Inserting WordArt into a Document... 180	Moving Information 132
Linking Text Boxes............................. 186	Outline Commands 130
Text Wrapping.................................... 186	Outlining an Existing Document 130
Hard Spacing... 33	Promote and Demote Information 131
Header and Footer 42	Outlined Numbered List 134
Moving between Sections 68	Page Setup 43
Highlighting Information in a Document .. 26	Paper Tab 44
Hyperlinks... 175	Paste Special 174
Creating a Hyperlink in a Document .169	PDF Document 16
Creating a Hyperlink to a Web Page. 167	Picture Watermarks 163
Deleting a Hyperlink 169	Plagiarism 92
Edit a Hyperlink 168	Print Layout View 12
Indent Icons 70	Print Preview 45
Index... 193	Printing... 45
Indexes	Promote Information 131
Creating an Index 89	Protection... 146
Insert Table Feature 55	Quick Access Toolbar............................. 10
Join Cells 54	Ribbon.. 11
Labels 114, 121	Rotating Text... 63
Letters 104	Rows 53, 54
Macros 175	Save a Document as a PDF 16
Deleting a Macro 161	Saving a Document................................ 14
Record a Macro 156	Section Breaks.. 65

Shadows 181
Shortcut Keys 79, 192
Spell and Grammar Facility 24
   Adding Words to the Dictionary 25
   Grammar Check Facility 25
Styles 75, 83
   Adding a Style to a Template 78
   Assign a Shortcut Key to a Style 79
   Automatic Update Feature 78
   Creating a New Style 78
   Deleting a Style from a Template 81
   Displaying Styles in a Document 75
   Modifying a Style 76
   Working with Styles 76
Subdocuments 136
Sub-Folders 14
Tab Stop Marker
   Different Tab and Indent Icons 70
   Identify the Tab Stop Marker 70
   Removing Tabs from the Ruler 71
   Setting Tabs from the Ruler 70
   Setting Tabs from the Tab Dialog Box 71
Table Grouping Commands 52
Table of Contents 4, 88, 133, 162
   Creating a Table of Contents 86
Table Styles 59
Tables
   AutoFit Feature 59
   AutoFormat Feature 59
   Deleting a Table Style 62
   Deleting Columns 54
   Deleting Rows 54
   Drawing Pencil 62
   Insert Table Feature 55
   Inserting Columns 53
   Inserting Rows 53
   Merge or Join Cells 54
   Rotating Text in a Table 63

Table Grouping Commands 52
Tabs 70, 74
Templates 81
   Open and Amend an existing Template 125
   Save a Document as a Template 122
   View a Template 124
Text Boxes 185
Text Form Fields 140, 142
Text Watermarks 164
Text Wrap 41
Text Wrapping 186
Tour of the Word Screen 10
   Draft View 12
   File Tab 10
   Full Screen Reading View 12
   Help 11
   Outline View 12
   Print Layout View 12
   Quick Access Toolbar 10
   Ribbon 11
   Ruler 11
   Scroll Bars 11
   Status Bar 12
   Title Bar 11
   Web Layout View 12
   Zoom Control 11
Track Changes
   How to use Track Changes 99
Undo and Redo Facility 25
Watermarks 166
   Delete a Watermark 165
   Picture Watermarks 163
   Text Watermark 164
Web Layout View 12
Window/Orphan Control 41
WordArt 180, 181
Zoom Control 11